The Pros and Cons
25 Topics for Adult ESL Students to Build Fluency

Ashley Shawn Wilkes

The Pros and Cons: 25 Engaging Topics for Adult ESL Students (1st Edition)
Writen and designed by Ashley Shawn Wilkes
https://www.linkedin.com/in/shawnwilkes/

Based on the PowerPoint presentations from www.ESLPPT.com.

© 2019 Ashley Shawn Wilkes

All rights reserved. This book or parts thereof may not be reproduced in any form, stored in any retrieval system, or transmitted in any form by any means—electronic, mechanical, photocopy, recording, or otherwise—without prior written permission of the publisher.
For permissions contact: shawn.wilkes@eslppt.com.

For information about special discounts available for bulk purchases and sales promotions, contact ESLPPT at sales@eslppt.com.

All pictures provided by Pexels.com.

Using this Workbook

*Though the title of this workbook is **The Pros and Cons**, that is simply referring to the unifying feature of opening each unit with a discussion of the pros and cons of that unit's particular topic. This opening discussion is something of a warm-up activity to get students thinking a bit about the topic of the class, which will allow them to be able to participate in the other activities of the unit with more ease.*

This workbook can be used with a student one-on-one, as well as with pairs and groups. As such, most of the instructions have been left a bit vague regarding whether the student should work alone or not. This is entirely up to the teacher. However, whenever you can have students work together, it is recommended that you do so, as this will maximize the STT (Student Talk Time) and minimize the TTT (Teacher Talk Time), which is the goal of any fluency-building endeavor.

Another important note is that this workbook can be flexible in terms of class duration and preparation. I've done classes where we've spent one hour on a particular unit, and there have also been classes where we've spent two hours on a unit. This really depends on two factors: how engaged your students are, and how much of the content you need to, or plan to, preteach before the students do the activities. If your students are really talkative, and engaged in a particular activity, I'd recommend giving them extra time if you can. If you have longer classes, you may also choose to preteach some information from the unit at the beginning of the class, but if you have shorter classes, you may have the students preview the unit at home.

With that said, I will try to give a bit of general advice on how you can approach the activities in this workbook. The information given is how I go about my classes, so it's based on my style of teaching. You'll likely have a different way of doing things, but this may give you some new ideas.

The Opening Question

Open the class by pairing off the students, and then having them discuss the opening pros and cons question for a short time. To facilitate discussion, and push the students to give more, you may set a goal for each pair to come up with a minimum of three pros and three cons. Following this, you can have students pair up with a new partner and share their answers, or elicit a few answers as a class if you are short on time.

Vocabulary Introduction

If possible, I would advise having the students preview the vocabulary before class. This will allow you to save class time, and spend more time on the discussion questions and activities. Please note that if you do have the students preview the vocabulary before class, be sure to elicit a few examples of sentences using the vocabulary from the students in order to check that they did preview, and do understand the words.

With that in mind, please refer to the vocabulary section at the end of the book. This section is meant to let you, and the students know, about the vocabulary within each unit that may be a bit tricky. By checking this section ahead of time, students will be able to follow the activities more smoothly, and the students will be able to talk with and engage each other more easily.

If you choose to introduce the vocabulary in class, try to use the example sentences and pictures to have the students guess the meaning of each word before explaining it yourself. You can have them do this in groups or pairs, which will allow them to help each other and speak more. Once you've given them a bit of time to discover the meaning of the words for themselves, elicit some definitions and examples from the students to check for understanding.

Discussion Questions

If you have a smaller class, or talkative students, then pairing off the students and having them discuss the questions is a good way to go, as it will maximize STT. However, if you have a larger class with several students who may be shy or quiet, you may want to create larger groups, and mix in the more talkative students with the quieter students. This may help get some of the quieter students to come out of their shells, and will be a good opportunity for some of the more active students to take on leadership roles. As the students begin discussing the questions, pay attention to if they are reading all of the questions at once, or are reading the questions one-by-one and talking after each question. If they are reading all of the questions at once, and trying to understand them completely, they may run out of time before having even discussed the first question. So, it is advisable to make sure the students approach the discussion question-by-question.

Once enough time has been given for the students to discuss the questions, you can either have the students as a class share a few ideas, if you have a shorter class, or mix up the pairs or groups and have them report what they discussed with their previous partner(s), if you have a longer class.

Critical Thinking Activities

These activities are meant to have the students think more deeply about the topic, or weigh choices and consequences if they were placed in a difficult situation. The activities are not meant to have an easy or direct answer.

These activities tend to be doable as individual thinking activities that lead into the sharing and comparing of answers, or as group activities where the members must come to a consensus. This may be ideal for larger groups of students, as each student can report his or her reasoning to the class, which may lead into an opportunity for extended discussion or debate. However, this is also doable for smaller-size classes if you allow the students to work on the activities individually first, and then come together to share their ideas.

Collaborative Activities

The collaborative activities generally focus on students working together to create something. This is achieved by answering the provided questions and coming up with specific details; such as creating a schedule, planning a budget or assigning chores. Students must discuss the options and come to a consensus on what they want to do.

These activities tend to be a bit longer in nature, so if one is included within a unit, I would advise spending a minimum of 20 minutes on it. If you are doing a collaborative activity in a two-hour class, you can extend the activity by having the groups reform with new members, and then have them discuss and compromise on the choices they made with their previous groups.

Statistics & Statistics Discussion

Every unit will include 1-3 statistics at the end of it, with some questions based on them. I would recommend having the students read the questions individually, and then asking them how they felt about the statistics, as some of the statistics may be a bit surprising to them. They can discuss this question as a class, or within groups. Once they've had time to discuss this question, have them dive into the statistics discussion questions.

Please note that I've endeavored to use verified statistics where I could, but it is important to take them with a grain of salt. The point of the statistics is to get the students talking about different ideas and viewpoints. With that in mind, I would let the students know this ahead of time.

Extension Activities and Closing

Every unit closes with either an extended discussion, agree or disagree activity or a minor collaborative activity. These are meant to be considered "warm down" activities that will allow the students to reflect on their ideas, and whether or not that have changed, during the course of the topic.

You can wrap up this section by asking the students one of the three following questions:

   01.   What did you learn from this unit?
   02.   Did anything surprise you in this unit?
   03.   Have any of your ideas changed during this unit?

Tips for Teachers

Some teachers using this workbook may be new to ESL, or just new to teaching ESL to adults. As such, I would like to endeavor to provide some tips that have served me well over the years, and will make your classes flow more smoothly, as well as help students to make much more progress. Please keep in mind that you might need to tweak them a bit based on your situation.

1. Set the Framework

Some of the topics and activities in this workbook deal with issues that may be a bit sensitive to some people. You know your audience, and you should identify what topics they will be comfortable discussing, and what topics that they may have a slight aversion to.

When you identify a topic that may cause discomfort to some students, then it is important to mentally prepare the students before you jump in. If you open the class, or course, with an explanation that the views in this workbook represent one perspective, and that they are just meant to challenge students to get them talking, they are more likely to be mentally prepared, and approach the topics with a more open mind. Explain the alternate viewpoint first in order to minimize shock. Once the shock aspect has been minimized, the students will be less likely to be offended.

This technique can be applied to a variety of situations with your students. For example, if you have a habit of joking a lot in class, or you have a personality that is a bit different from what students typically expect, you can set the framework the first time you meet the students by letting them know exactly who you are, and what they can expect from you. This tactic can lead to a sharp decline in misunderstandings in settings where there are different cultural backgrounds. Setting the framework is probably the most important tip I can give any new teacher.

2. Have Students Preview the Material

This is especially useful if you plan to cover a unit in one hour. If students can preview the new vocabulary, and think about the activities and discussion questions ahead of time, then more class time can be devoted to having the students engage each other and practice more.

However, keep in mind that it is still important to check for understanding at the beginning of the class. Some students may not have previewed sufficiently, or may think they understand a question, but their understanding may not be accurate. Use concept checking questions (CCQs) to check for understanding.

3. Concept Checking Questions

How do you know if a student understands the meaning of a word? The first instinct that many teachers have is to ask, "Do you understand?" Unfortunately, this question doesn't tell you anything. This is where CCQs come in. CCQs allow you to evaluate if the student correctly understands the information or not. They are the bread and butter of any teacher. Imagine that you just taught the word 'ban', and you want to know whether or not the students understand this word. You could check by asking, "Does ban mean to allow or not allow something" or you could ask a more open question like, "What are some items that are banned in an airport?" Either of these questions will more explicitly let you know whether or not a student really understands the word or not.

4. Expect More, Get More

Many students may have a habit of giving short answers, or not providing additional information without being coaxed. With this in mind, set higher goals for the students. If you have strong students, give them a minimum word count for their answers during an activity or discussion. For my intermediate level students, I tend to require them to give me sentences of eight words at the minimum, and advanced students are required to sometimes give twelve words at the minimum.

You can also encourage students to always ask follow-up questions in response to new information, or prompt students with "because" when they give you answers.

By expecting more, and requiring students to give you more, they will progress much more quickly in developing their fluency. It will be a challenge at first, but students will become accustomed to it.

5. Be a Facilitator

The role of a teacher is to teach, which means the teacher will spend a significant amount of time talking. When the teacher talks more, the students talk less. When the students talk less, they make less progress with the language. With that said, a degree of teaching is necessary for students who are just starting out with the language, but as students progress and move to higher levels, which is the target audience of this workbook, it becomes more about allowing the students to use the language, with the teacher acting as a facilitator and guide. Aim for around 80% STT if possible. Open the class by introducing a few new words and phrases that might be useful, set up the activity or activities, and then give the students free rein. Listen in on their conversations during the activities in this workbook, and provide feedback and guidance as needed.

6. Elicit Self- and Peer-Correct

It's natural for teachers to step in and try to correct students when they make mistakes, but it's actually not very helpful. Quickly given, quickly forgotten. Instead, when you hear a student make a mistake with the language, it's helpful to repeat what the student said, but highlight the mistake by raising your voice to a higher pitch, and looking confused. This will let the student know that something is incorrect, and encourage the student to self-correct, or be peer-corrected by his or her classmates. By having students correct themselves, they will be more likely to grow from the mistake, as well as gain confidence since they are able to correct their own mistakes.

Tips for Students

If you are a student using this workbook, you probably already have a pretty good foundation of English. However, whether you are just beginning to learn English, or are a veteran student, the following are a few general tips to help you build your fluency more quickly, and maintain it. My students who have followed these tips have shown the greatest amount of progress in the shortest periods of time. These tips can be challenging, but will help you make much more progress.

1. Make an English-Only Pact

If you only use English in the classroom, or with a teacher, it will never feel natural speaking English. Ask one of your classmates or friends who is also learning English to make an English-only pact with you. This is where you both agree to only speak English to each other inside or outside of class. By speaking only English with this person, you will be forced to use English in a variety of real world situations, and speaking English will start to feel more natural to you.

2. Always Offer More

Always give more information. If someone asks you about your last holiday, don't just say it was good; explain why it was good, and what you did on your holiday. The more information you provide, the more you are practicing expressing your ideas, and recalling vocabulary.

3. Turn Off the Subtitles

A good way to build up your listening fluency is by watching sitcoms or dramas. Movies are okay, but TV shows tend to use more natural language. Sitcoms are especially useful, because they are topical, use casual language, are funny and quite short. You can save a few episodes of your favorite sitcom on your smartphone, and watch them during the daily commute to work, or elsewhere. However, it is best to turn off the subtitles. By leaving the subtitles on, you will focus more on reading than listening, which will have very little benefit to your listening skills. If you are watching a show and can't understand a phrase after listening two or three times, then turn on the subtitles just for that part of the show.

4. Change Your Thinking Language

Many students often complain that they have no opportunity to practice speaking English, but that's actually not true. How often do you go outside and think about the weather? Do you sometimes think of other things will brushing your teeth or taking a shower? Change your thinking language to English, and force yourself to speak your thoughts out loud. This will allow you to eventually start speaking naturally and directly, without internally translating first.

5. Teach Others

In class, volunteer to help others, or to be the leader of your group for that class. Put yourself in a situation where you will have to help and teach others. Doing so will force you to organize your ideas in a different way, as well as think of examples that will help your classmates. The best way to learn is to teach.

6. Speak, Don't Just Listen

Maybe you like to watch football, and you watch football often. However, does watching football mean that you can play football well? If you want to play football well, you have to get on the field and practice. The same is true of learning a new language. You can watch hundreds of shows and movies, and listen to music and podcasts, but you have to open your mouth and use the language. You have to speak to succeed.

7. Be Comfortable Not Knowing

Some students want to understand every word in a sentence, and will spend a lot of time focusing on the words they don't understand. When they do this, they will not pay attention to the overall meaning of the sentence, and will fall behind in the conversation or class. It's okay to not understand every word, and it's okay to guess. Be comfortable not understanding everything. You'll make mistakes, but you will also make more progress, because you will be speaking out and participating more.

8. Put Aside the Dictionary

Dictionaries and translation tools can be useful, but be careful to not use them too much. Easily learned, easily forgotten. If you are trying to express an idea, but don't know a certain word, try to explain your idea in a different way, or explain the word that you want to use. This will allow you to become more flexible with the language, as well as help you recall vocabulary that you learned before.

9. It's a Process. Stay Motivated.

This bit of advice is something I usually tell new students at my school who don't have a strong foundation in English. However, I think it is also helpful to remind you advanced learners: learning anything is a process, and is gradual. Imagine that you want to lose weight, so you go to the gym and start exercising. Each day, there will be small changes in your body, but because the process is gradual, you don't see those small changes. Yet, your body is changing and improving. The same is true of learning. Keep speaking out as much as possible, and keep your motivation for learning in mind. You are getting better and making progress, so stick with it.

Table of Contents

Information

1	Using This Workbook
4	Tips for Teachers
6	Tips for Students
160	Vocabulary Bank
166	Statistics Sources

All images used in this workbook are courtesy of Pexels.com and the amazing photographers who contribute their works to Pexels.

Units

10	Arranged Marriages
16	Helping the Poor
22	Telling White Lies
28	War
34	Adoption
40	Colonizing Mars
46	An International One-Child Policy
52	Living Together Before Marriage
58	Dating a Colleague
64	Moving Abroad
70	Being Child-free
76	Cloning
82	Dating During High School
88	Making Kids Earn Their Allowance
94	Banning Smoking
100	Going Completely Green in 5 Years
106	Nuclear Weapons and Energy
112	Open International Immigration
118	Marrying Outside of Your Culture
124	Harsher Punishments
130	Dating Students
136	Being Your Own Boss
142	Divorce
148	Dating Apps
154	Using Tablets Instead of Textbooks

Unit 01 — Arranged Marriages

What do you think are the pros and cons of arranged marriages?

Vocabulary and Discussion

Stable
My husband and I have a stable life. It doesn't change much.

Attraction
I was physically attracted to him, but we didn't have much in common.

Passion
The passion has died. We don't even sleep in the same bed anymore.

Arrogant
The king was arrogant and looked down upon the common people.

Personality
It's difficult to have a conversation with someone who is too shy.

Abusive
My husband was physically abusive, so I left him and went to the police.

Discussion Questions

Discuss the following questions with a partner. Be prepared to share your answers.

01. Are you married or in a relationship?
02. Would you ever consider an arranged marriage?
03. At what age would you consider an arranged marriage to be a good choice for you?
04. Do you think that love is really necessary in a marriage?
05. Do you believe that love can grow between two strangers?

First Impressions

Discussion Activity

Imagine that you are a 24-year-old woman from a very traditional family. Arranged marriages are common in your culture, and most people get married by the time they are in their mid-20s. Recently, your parents have been worried that you will not get married and have children. You agree to marry someone that they introduce to you. They arrange for you to meet three men, and you agree to marry one of them.

What's your first impression of each man? Who would you be most likely to choose? Who would you be least likely to choose? Share your ideas with a partner.

Man A

Age: 32
Sign: Sagittarius
Job: Shop Manager

Works 40 hours a week.
Earns $2,000USD per month.

He is a man with very little passion. He'll be kind to you, but he prefers to spend his time at bars and going to karaoke with his friends. He has a stable job, but little opportunity to progress.

Man B

Age: 23
Sign: Virgo
Job: Salesman

Works 30 hours a week.
Earns $3,000USD per month.

He is not very clever, and is quite lazy and childish. However, he is good at sales, and his job has potential if he can motivate himself to try harder. When he is not working, he is either sleeping or playing games.

Man C

Age: 45
Sign: Aries
Job: Businessman

Works 60+ hours a week.
Earns $10,000USD per month.

He is very arrogant, but also very intelligent. He's a playboy, and believes that buying expensive gifts is enough to keep a woman happy. He would want you to stay home and be a housewife.

Pros and Cons

Who's the Best Choice?

Critical Thinking

Discuss the questions below with a partner. Come to an agreement about which man would be the best choice and why.

01. What are the pros of marrying each man?

    A   B   C

    _____   _____   _____

    _____   _____   _____

    _____   _____   _____

02. What are the cons of marrying each man?

    A   B   C

    _____   _____   _____

    _____   _____   _____

    _____   _____   _____

03. What would your life be like in 10 years if you married each man?

    A   B   C

    _____   _____   _____

    _____   _____   _____

    _____   _____   _____

Who's the best choice? _____

Difficult Choices

Critical Thinking

Read the following situation, then consider each problem. What would you do if you met the same problems? Make a few notes, and then discuss your answers with your partner or group.

For these choices, let's imagine that you decided to marry Man A three years ago. After the wedding, he got a promotion and now earns more money. Your relationship has never been very passionate, but it has been stable. You have a 2-year-old son with him.

He is not at home as much recently. He said he has a lot of work to do, but you later find out that he has a girlfriend that he sees several times a week.

Problem 1: What do you do?

You decide to stay with him and ignore the fact that he has a girlfriend. Your son is only two, and you are worried about what your parents might say, so you don't want to divorce. However, at work, you meet a man who likes you, and you are also attracted to him.

Problem 2: What do you do?

You decide to date the man at work. His name is James, and you are happy with him. You feel like you love James, but you are not sure if the relationship can last. Your husband finds out about your relationship, and is threatening to tell your parents and divorce you.

Problem 3: What do you do?

Statistics and Discussion

On average, the man in an arranged marriage is 4.5 years older than the woman.

Only 6.3% of arranged marriages end in divorce.

46.4% of arranged marriages in South Asia are to girls who are under the age of 18.

Check "Statistics Sources" in the back of the workbook for additional information.

Statistics Discussion

Discuss the following questions with a partner.

01. Why do you think it is less common for people in arranged marriages to divorce?
02. What do you think is an acceptable age difference in an arranged marriage?
03. When should people be allowed to marry legally?

Extended Discussion

Discuss the following questions with a partner. Be prepared to share your answers.

01. Do you believe that it is important for your parents to approve of who you marry?
02. Would you agree to marry someone if you had no physical attraction to him or her?
03. What would you do if the person you married became abusive emotionally or physically?
04. Have any of your ideas about arranged marriages changed during this lesson?

Unit 02 Helping the Poor

What do you think are the pros and cons of helping poor people by giving them money?

Vocabulary and Discussion

Low-income

Low-income families are often not able to send their children to college.

Soup Kitchen

Soup kitchens provide free, hot meals to people in need.

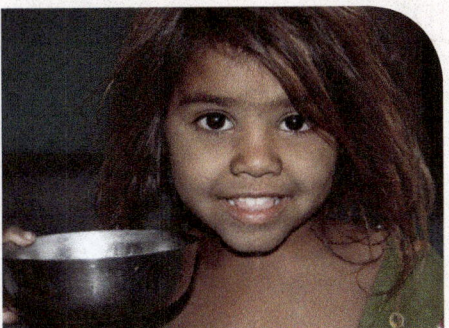

Poverty

Many families in poverty are unable to have three meals a day.

Foreclosure

The bank foreclosed on my home since I was unable to repay my loan.

Citizen

It's the responsibility of every citizen to pay taxes.

Paycheck-to-Paycheck

Since my wife lost her job, we are living paycheck-to-paycheck.

Discussion Questions

Discuss the following questions with a partner. Be prepared to share your answers.

01. Have you ever given money to a beggar? If so, explain the situation.
02. Other than giving money, what are some other ways to help beggars?
03. Do most beggars really need to beg, or are they able to work and just choose not to?
04. In many countries, children beg. What can be done to help them?
05. Do you think it is possible for you to become a beggar in the future?

The Sick Spouse

Discussion Activity

In the United States, many families live paycheck-to-paycheck, and are afraid of becoming sick. If they become sick, they will have to miss work. This means that they will lose money needed to pay bills and put food on the table. They may also have to borrow money from a bank to pay overly expensive hospital bills.

Imagine that you are in a lower-middle class family. You make enough money each month to survive, but not enough money to save. You and your spouse have two children. Your extended family is unable to help you. Your spouse gets sick and has to go to the hospital. Your spouse will not be able to work for several months, and you have very little money saved in the bank. What options do you have?

Work with a partner to make a list of five ways that you would deal with this problem.

Consider the following when answering choosing your five solutions:

- *Is it possible for a lower-income family to do it?*
- *Can it be done without the help of the extended family?*
- *Will it cause harm to the children?*

1. _____
2. _____
3. _____
4. _____
5. _____

 Always try to give more information in your answers. Instead of saying, "My trip to Thailand was good," try to say, "My trip to Thailand was good, because the weather was nice and the people were friendly."

Difficult Choices

Critical Thinking

Read the following situation, then consider each problem. What would you do if you met the same problems? Make a few notes, and then discuss your answers with your partner or group.

For these choices, let's imagine that your spouse is still in the hospital. In the past, you borrowed money from the bank to help buy a house and a car. Now, you've borrowed more money to pay hospital bills. You are behind on your payments. Your friends and family are also lower-middle class, and unable to help you financially.

It has already been more than a month, and your spouse is still not well enough to work. Because you have been unable to pay the bank back, the bank is threatening to foreclose on your home. If this happens, you will be homeless.

Problem 1: What do you do?

_____
_____
_____
_____

The bank has foreclosed on your home, and you and your family have been living in your car for a week, because there are no homeless shelters in your city. Because you are living in your car, your spouse's illness is becoming worse again.

Problem 2: What do you do?

_____
_____
_____
_____

Due to the poor living conditions, the government wants to take your children away and put them in a foster home. If this happens, it may be several months or years before you are able to get your children back.

Problem 3: What do you do?

_____
_____
_____
_____

Helping the Poor

A New Program

Collaborative Activity

Your city wants to test a new program to help low-income families and reduce poverty. There are five different ideas to choose from, and each program has pros and cons.

Read the following situation, then discuss the pros and cons of each idea with a partner. Finally, choose which idea you believe is the best choice for your city, and which idea is the worst choice for your city.

01. Create a program to help unemployed citizens find jobs.

    Pros: _____

    Cons: _____

02. Open soup kitchens to serve food to homeless and low-income citizens.

    Pros: _____

    Cons: _____

03. Build low-cost housing.

    Pros: _____

    Cons: _____

04. All citizens will receive a basic income to cover basic food and housing expenses.

    Pros: _____

    Cons: _____

05. Create education programs to help low-income and homeless citizens learn skills needed to find new jobs.

    Pros: _____

    Cons: _____

Best Choice		Worst Choice	

Statistics and Discussion

Every year in India, up to 60,000 children are taken from their families and forced to beg.[2]

Only about 20% of the beggars arrested in the United Kingdom are homeless.[1]

A man in China earned $40,000USD in one year by forcing children to beg for him.[3]

Check "Statistics Sources" in the back of the workbook for additional information.

Statistics Discussion

Discuss the following questions with a partner.

01. How do you feel about people who are not homeless begging?
02. What should citizens do when they see a child begging?
03. What should be done to stop the abduction and selling of children?

Agree or Disagree

Do you agree or disagree with the following statements?

01. Most poor people are lazy.
02. Most poor people are uneducated.
03. The government has a responsibility to help poor people.
04. Citizens have a responsibility to help poor people.

Unit 03 — Telling White Lies

What do you think are the pros and cons of telling white lies?

Vocabulary and Discussion

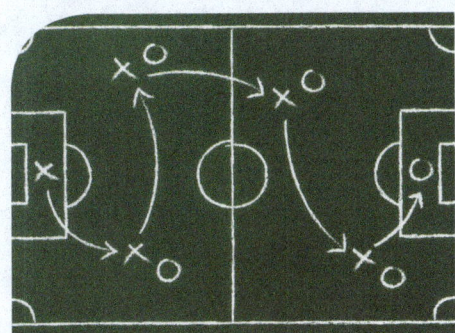

Tactful

Instead of being direct, think first and say it in a tactful way.

Fib

Children will often tell a small fib to get out of trouble.

Acquaintance

I only met him a couple of times. He's just an acquaintance of mine.

Dating Profile

My dating profile says I am tall, but I am really just average height.

Betray

When someone lies to you, you may feel betrayed and not trust them.

Exaggerate

Men often exaggerate about the size of the fish they catch.

Discussion Questions

Discuss the following questions with a partner. Be prepared to share your answers.

01. When's the last time you told a white lie?
02. When's the last time you think someone told you a white lie?
03. What impact does a white lie have on a relationship?
04. When do you think telling a white lie is the right thing to do?
05. Is there a time that you wish someone had told you a white lie instead of being honest?

Tactful Honesty

Discussion Activity

Many people believe that white lies are helpful, and can help people feel better, as well as avoid embarrassment. However, a lie is a lie, and it can damage trust in a relationship. Imagine that you have decided to be completely honest in your life, and never lie again.

Read the following situations in which people commonly tell white lies. What's the best way to be honest in each situation?

01. Your child often gets bad grades at school, and thinks he is not smart.

    _____

    _____

02. Your girlfriend or wife asks you if she looks fat in a new pair of pants she bought.

    _____

    _____

03. Your 6-year-old child asks you where babies come from.

    _____

    _____

04. Your boyfriend says he loves you for the first time, and asks if you love him. You care about him, but don't feel like you love him yet.

    _____

    _____

05. After work, you went out for drinks with an ex at a bar. You come home and your spouse asks where you've been.

    _____

    _____

Common Lies

Discussion Activity

What are five common lies that parents tell their children? What's the best way to be honest in each situation?

What's the lie?	How to be honest tactfully?
01. _____	_____
02. _____	_____
03. _____	_____
04. _____	_____
05. _____	_____

What are five common lies that people tell their romantic partners? What's the best way to be honest in each situation?

What's the lie?	How to be honest tactfully?
01. _____	_____
02. _____	_____
03. _____	_____
04. _____	_____
05. _____	_____

Extended Discussion

01. Have you ever told, or been told, any of those lies?
02. Would you prefer to be lied to, or receive some tactful honesty?
03. Which of the lies above do you think is the worst?

FLUENCY TIP! Translation tools can be useful sometimes, but be careful not to overuse them. If you don't know a word, find another way to explain what you want to say. This develops your language creativity, and helps you remember old vocabulary.

The Perfect Lie

Discussion Activity

What's the perfect white lie to tell in each of the following situations?

1 A police officer pulls you over for speeding.

2 You forget your girlfriend's birthday.

3 You don't want to give someone your social media information.

4 An old acquaintance is in town and wants to hang out, but you really don't want to.

5 You are late for work, and your boss calls you.

6 You go to your friend's home for dinner. Her husband cooks, and it tastes terrible.

7 Your grandmother gives you a horrible-looking sweater. Later, she asks why you never wear it.

8 You forget to send out an important e-mail at work.

9 Your young child asks where babies come from.

FLUENCY TIP! We always talk to ourselves. Sometimes we say, "Ah, the weather is so nice today," or "I am so hungry." Try switching your internal language to English. By pushing yourself to think in English, you will begin to speak out more quickly.

Statistics and Discussion

About 40% of adults lie on their resumes. 90% of adults lie on dating websites.*

About 90% of children know the concept of lying by the age of four.*

In a 10 minute conversation, 60% of adults will tell a lie.*

Check "Statistics Sources" in the back of the workbook for additional information.

Statistics Discussion

Discuss the following questions with a partner.

01. Since the kids learned it from them, can parents really be angry at their kids for lying?
02. Have your ever lied to get a job?
03. Would you date someone if you found out that he or she lied on his or her dating profile?

Agree or Disagree

Do you agree or disagree with the following statements?

01. You can't trust someone who lies to you.
02. People are more honest chatting online than face-to-face.
03. You have to lie when you first start dating someone.
04. Parents should always be honest with their children, no matter what.

Unit 04 War

What do you think are the pros and cons of war?

Vocabulary and Discussion

Casualty

During WWII, there were 40 million civilian casualties.

Punish

If you harm a person, you will be sent to prison as punishment.

Sanctions

Economic sanctions were placed on the country due to war crimes.

Counterattack

He swung at me, and then I knocked him out with my counterattack.

Ally

America and England were allies during WWII.

Embargo

Part of the sanctions on the country was a trade embargo.

Discussion Questions

Discuss the following questions with a partner. Be prepared to share your answers.

01. What are some reasons that people go to war?
02. Do you think any of those reasons are good?
03. Do you believe that war can lead to peace?
04. In what ways can war help a country develop?
05. Would you be willing to serve your country in a war?

Rules of War

Discussion Activity

A major war has just ended, and during the war, there were many civilian casualties. As a result, many countries have asked the United Nations to create 10 new rules of war, as well as punishments for violating those rules of war. Imagine that you represent the United Nations Council of War Crimes, and it is your job to create the new rules and punishments.

Create 10 rules of war. Make notes in the spaces provided, but focus on speaking out.

Rule 01 _____

Rule 02 _____

Rule 03 _____

Rule 04 _____

Rule 05 _____

Rule 06 _____

Rule 07 _____

Rule 08 _____

Rule 09 _____

Rule 10 _____

The Punishments

Critical Thinking

Decide on how individuals and governments should be punished for violating each of the new rules of war. Make notes in the spaces provided, and be prepared to share your answers.

Punishments for Individuals	Punishments for Governments
01. _____	_____
02. _____	_____
03. _____	_____
04. _____	_____
05. _____	_____
06. _____	_____
07. _____	_____
08. _____	_____
09. _____	_____
10. _____	_____

War   Page 31

Decision Points

Critical Thinking

Imagine that you are council members of the country of Andor. You have just received news that a close ally of yours, Shara, has violated the rules of war created by the United Nations. You have been allied with Shara for more than 25 years, and you have a strong trade relationship with them.

Read the following problems. Consider what your country should do in each situation.

Several countries in the UN are now calling for an embargo against Shara. If you agree with them, Shara will become your enemy. If you don't agree, the other countries in the UN may become your enemy. What's your choice?

You have decided to agree with the UN. Now, Shara has stopped trading with you. As a result, unemployment increases rapidly in your country, and the economy declines. How do you deal with this?

The increased public unrest has forced you to try to direct the public's anger towards Shara. You decide to declare war. How do you start the war?

You launch a surprise attack and destroy several of Shara's military bases. Now, they have launched a counterattack and bombed several public schools and hospitals. How do you respond?

You have discovered that another ally, Altara, is selling weapons to Shara. What action do you take?

Statistics and Discussion

One source claims that 14,500 wars have taken place between 3500 BC and today, costing 3.5 billion lives, and leaving only 300 years of peace.*

The earliest evidence of war was found at a 14,000-year-old cemetery. About 45% percent of the skeletons there displayed signs of violent death.*

Check "Statistics Sources" in the back of the workbook for additional information.

Statistics Discussion

Discuss the following questions with a partner.

01. Do you believe humans are capable of peace?
02. What do you think people 14,000 years ago fought over?
03. What do you think has been the most common cause of the 14,500 wars?

Extended Discussion

Discuss the following questions with a partner. Be prepared to share your answers.

01. What are some reasons that people would choose to be a soldier?
02. What do you think is most difficult about being a soldier?
03. Do you think military service should be required for all citizens?
04. What do you think "might is right" means? Do you agree or disagree with this phrase?

Unit 05 — Adoption

What do you think are the pros and cons of adoption?

Vocabulary and Discussion

Orphan

She became an orphan after both of her parents died in the accident.

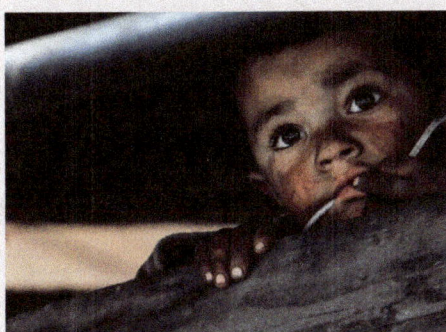

Timid

He's very timid around other children. He's quiet and stays alone.

Abandon

The home was abandoned after the flood. No one's been there for years.

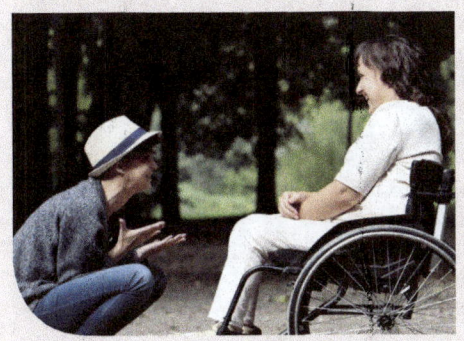

Disabled

If you injure your back, you may become disabled and unable to walk.

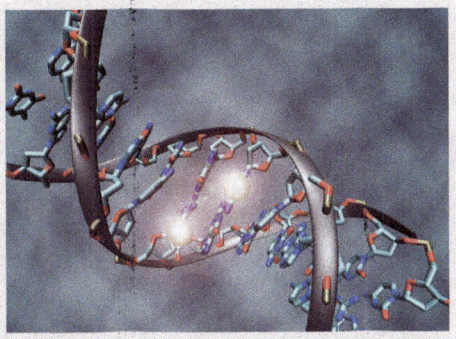

Genes

You can make fruit resistant to insects by editing its genes.

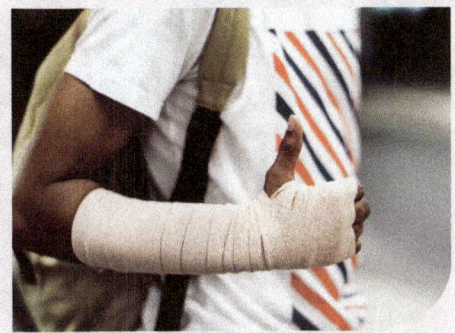

Recover

It will take a couple of months for my broken arm to recover.

Discussion Questions

Discuss the following questions with a partner. Be prepared to share your answers.

01. How would you feel if you found out that you were adopted?
02. Would you ever consider adopting a child?
03. Would you consider adopting a child with a physical or mental disability?
04. How long do you think it takes a child to become used to a new family and environment?
05. Other than adoption, what are some other ways that orphans can be helped?

Making a Choice

Discussion Activity

Imagine that you and your spouse cannot have children, so you decide to adopt. You have narrowed your choices down to four children. Which child will you choose to adopt and why?

Read the following profiles. Together with a partner, come to an agreement on which child to adopt. Be prepared to explain your logic.

Name: Jonathan   Age: 5   Nationality: American

Jonathan has been in the orphanage for two years. His parents died in a car accident two years ago, and no one in his family wanted him. In the accident, his body was severely scarred. He's very shy and quiet.

Name: Xiao   Age: 8   Nationality: Chinese

Xiao's mother died during childbirth, and her father died from cancer three months ago. She was often beaten by her father, so she is afraid of men, and is timid. She has never attended school.

Name: Vincent   Age: 2   Nationality: Brazilian

Vincent was born with one leg, and abandoned at birth. He has been in the orphanage his entire life. He doesn't play with the other children at the orphanage. He is a quiet, but very intelligent child.

Name: Tabby   Age: 3   Nationality: Kenyan

Tabby's mother died from AIDS shortly after she was born, and her father died in a war before she was born. She has been in the orphanage her entire life. She is a bright, playful child.

Getting Adjusted

Critical Thinking

You chose to adopt Xiao, and you will go and pick her up from the orphanage in one week. However, before she comes, you need to make a plan for how to get her adjusted to living in your city or country. The better your plan is, the faster she will adapt, and the happier she will be.

Make a plan to help Xiao adjust to living in your city or country by answering the provided questions.

01. How should you prepare her room in order to make her feel comfortable?

02. What can be done to help her learn the local language?

03. When should you enroll her in school? What type of school? What grade?

04. How can you help her begin to make friends?

05. What can you do to help rebuild her trust in males?

Adoption

Difficult Choices

Critical Thinking

Read the following situation, then consider each problem. What would you do if you met the same problems? Make a few notes, and then discuss your answers with your partner or group.

For these choices, let's imagine that you decided to adopt Jonathan. You welcomed him into your home, and he seems very happy. He is beginning to laugh and play with other children.

One year after adopting Jonathan, you find out he has a genetic illness that is costly and long-term. Your family is lower-middle class, and you are afraid that you can't afford to help him.

Problem 1: What do you do?

You kept Jonathan, and helped him to recover from the illness. It was difficult, but your family became closer because of it. He is now nine, and his aunt has found him and wants to take him from you. She regrets not adopting him before, and blames her ex-husband.

Problem 2: What do you do?

You refused the aunt, and asked her to not come back, because you don't want to upset Jonathan. Now, it is 4 years later. He receives a letter from his aunt explaining what happened, and he is angry that you kept it a secret.

Problem 3: What do you do?

Pros and Cons

Statistics and Discussion

*About 5,000 children are adopted from China each year.**

*Girls are 64% likely to be adopted, compared to just 36% for boys.**

*In the past 30 years, about 250,000 children were adopted in the US.**

Check "Statistics Sources" in the back of the workbook for additional information.

Statistics Discussion

Discuss the following questions with a partner.

01. Why do you think so many families choose to adopt children from China?
02. Why are girls much more likely to be adopted than boys?
03. Do you think 250,000 children in 30 years is a large or small number? Explain.

Agree or Disagree

Do you agree or disagree with the following statements?

01. Instead of having a second child, families should first try to adopt.
02. Parents must be college-educated, or they should not be allowed to adopt.
03. People should only be allowed to adopt children from their own country.
04. It is impossible to love an adopted child as much as your own child.

Unit 06 Colonizing Mars

What do you think are the pros and cons of colonizing Mars?

Vocabulary and Questions

Rover

The Mars rover has sent back many amazing images of the landscape.

Colony

Mars One wants to have a colony of people on Mars by 2032.

Biodome

Living in a biodome would protect you from Mars' harsh environment.

Asteroid

An asteroid hit Earth 65 million years ago and killed the dinosaurs.

Shuttle

Space shuttles currently take several months to make the trip to Mars.

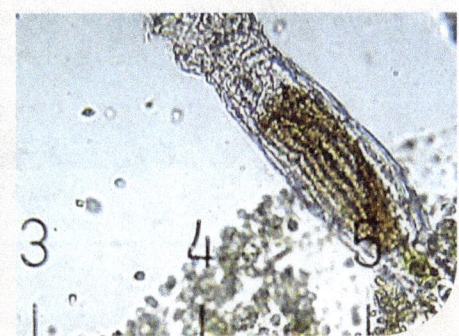

Microscopic Organism

Some scientists believe microscopic organisms once lived on Mars.

Discussion Questions

Discuss the following questions with a partner. Be prepared to share your answers.

01. Why do you believe some people want to colonize Mars?
02. In what year do you think humans will colonize Mars?
03. Do you think we should be spending a lot of money on trying to colonize Mars?
04. What type of person would be a good colonist to live on Mars?
05. Would you choose to be a colonist on Mars if given the chance?

Colonizing Mars

Collaborative Activity

You are the CEO of GalaxyX. Your company has developed a space shuttle that can go to Mars and return within 6 months. Your company has also developed a new biodome technology. This means you will be able to colonize Mars before the government, and create the first Martian colony!

Decide on a name for your colony.

Colony Name: _____

Every year, you will send 50 people to join the colony. Each person will spend 20 years there. Each year will have an objective that you need to achieve, so you need to choose the right people to send each year.

Answer the following questions in order to create a five-year plan for the colony. Each year, you can send 5 different "groups" of people. For example, you may send a group of agricultural scientists, a group of doctors, etc.

Example	Objective	Create a sustainable living environment.		
Group 1 10 Scientists	Group 2 15 Engineers	Group 3 10 Botanists	Group 4 5 Doctors	Group 5 10 Laborers

Year 1	Objective			
Group 1	Group 2	Group 3	Group 4	Group 5

Year 2	Objective			
Group 1	Group 2	Group 3	Group 4	Group 5

Year 3	Objective			
Group 1	Group 2	Group 3	Group 4	Group 5

Year 4	Objective			
Group 1	Group 2	Group 3	Group 4	Group 5

Year 5	Objective			
Group 1	Group 2	Group 3	Group 4	Group 5

The Comforts of Home

Discussion Activity

The Mars colony was established 20 years ago, and there are currently 2,000 people living there. Space shuttle technology has improved, and the trip to Mars can now be made in one month. GalaxyX has decided to build the first small market on Mars with 10 food and entertainment venues to keep the colonists happy.

Select which 10 food and entertainment venues should be built and why.

01. _____   _____
02. _____   _____
03. _____   _____
04. _____   _____
05. _____   _____
06. _____   _____
07. _____   _____
08. _____   _____
09. _____   _____
10. _____   _____

Colonizing Mars — Page 43

The End of Earth

Collaborative Activity

An asteroid has been discovered flying towards Earth. It is large enough to destroy all life on the planet, and it will impact in 7 days. There is only enough time to prepare one shuttle to send to the Mars colony. The Mars colony currently has 500 people on it, and is self-sustaining. The shuttle can carry four astronauts, as well as 10 additional people. Your team has been selected to choose which people will be saved, and you cannot choose yourselves, or your families. You have enough space on the shuttle to carry 10 small items as additional cargo, with each item weighing less than 5kg.

Choose which 10 people you believe need to be saved, as well as which 10 items should be sent as cargo.

Consider the following question: How will the people and items you choose help rebuild human civilization?

The 10 People to Save	The 10 Items to Send
01.	
02.	
03.	
04.	
05.	
06.	
07.	
08.	
09.	
10.	

Fluency TIP! Make an English-only pact with one of your classmates. If you force yourself to speak only English with this person inside and outside of class, you will be surprised at how much progress you make.

Statistics and Discussion

The Martian year is 1.88 Earth years, but it has seasons like Earth.*

If you go on a mission to Mars, you will be away from the Earth for 2.5 years.*

Mars One plans to have the first permanent colony on Mars by 2032.*

Check "Statistics Sources" in the back of the workbook for additional information.

Statistics Discussion

Discuss the following questions with a partner.

01. How do you think seasons on Mars would be different from seasons on Earth?
02. What would make you agree to be a colonist to Mars?
03. What's the longest period of time that you would accept being away from Earth?

Extended Discussion

Discuss the following questions with a partner. Be prepared to share your answers.

01. Some scientists believe that life on Earth may have come from Mars on an asteroid. Do you believe this is likely or not?
02. If it is proven that life on Earth comes from Mars, what would change for us?
03. Should we continue trying to explore space, or focus on fixing the problems on Earth?

Unit 07

An International One-Child Policy

What do you think are the pros and cons of an international one-child policy?

Vocabulary and Discussion

Aging Population

The aging population in Japan means some citizens retire later.

Dwindle

Resources are dwindling due to overpopulation.

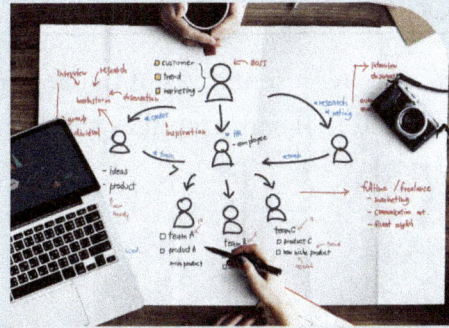

Condition

You can have the job if you meet the right conditions.

Imbalance

The one-child policy has created a gender imbalance in some countries.

Courtship

I tried to win her heart during a long courtship period.

Spoiled

The spoiled child was kicking and screaming in the supermarket.

Discussion Questions

Discuss the following questions with a partner. Be prepared to share your answers.

01. Do you think a one-child policy would be possible in your country?
02. Is it okay to ask people to not have more children in order to protect the environment?
03. How can you reduce the impact of an aging population?
04. Are children from one-child families more spoiled?
05. Do you think every country should agree to follow a one-child policy?

Conditions for a 2ⁿᵈ Child

Collaborative Activity

You are representatives of a government council. Your country has a one-child policy, but your government has decided that some families will be allowed to have a second child under certain conditions.

Create 10 conditions that would allow some families to have a second child. Make notes in the spaces provided, but focus on speaking out.

Condition 01 _____

Condition 02 _____

Condition 03 _____

Condition 04 _____

Condition 05 _____

Condition 06 _____

Condition 07 _____

Condition 08 _____

Condition 09 _____

Condition 10 _____

An Aging Population

Critical Thinking

Japan is facing the problem of an aging population due to low birthrates. As such, citizens are retiring later in life, and income from taxes is decreasing. Japan has introduced new immigration policies to attract skilled workers. This is to help rebalance the workforce, as well as increase tax revenues. Japan is also encouraging young couples to have more children,

Your country is now facing the same problem, and it's up to you to come up with ideas on how to boost the birthrate and attract immigration.

Create a plan to boost immigration to your country, as well as a plan to increase the birthrate.

The Plan to Increase Immigration

01. _____
02. _____
03. _____
04. _____
05. _____

The Plan to Increase the Birthrate

01. _____
02. _____
03. _____
04. _____
05. _____

An International One-Child Policy

Difficult Choices

Critical Thinking

Read the following situation, then consider each problem. What would you do if you met the same problems? Make a few notes, and then discuss your answers with your partner or group.

Imagine that your country has a one-child policy. If you violate it, you may pay a heavy fine, or go to prison. The government may even take away the second child when it is born. The government gives money to citizens who report families that violate the policy.

Even though you and your wife have been careful, your wife becomes pregnant again. If the government finds out that your wife is pregnant with a second child, you will both get in serious trouble.

Problem 1: What do you do?

_____
_____
_____
_____
_____

You decide to have the baby. Your wife quits her job and stays home so that no one will see her growing belly. Now, she is 6 months pregnant, and you think someone is going to report you both to the police.

Problem 2: What do you do?

_____
_____
_____
_____
_____

You sneak into a neighboring country to have the baby there. You and your wife want to return to your own country, but if you return, you might face arrest or other legal problems.

Problem 3: What do you do?

_____
_____
_____
_____
_____

Statistics and Discussion

In China, there will be 30 million more men than women in 2020, potentially leading to social instability, and courtship-motivated emigration.*

China's restrictions had a notable and long lasting impact on fertility rates, leading to well over 500 million averted births between 1970 and 2015.*

Check "Statistics Sources" in the back of the workbook for additional information.

Statistics Discussion

Discuss the following questions with a partner.

01. How would China be different today if the one-child policy had never happened there?
02. Why do you think there is such a gender imbalance in China?
03. What do you think China can do to address the gender imbalance?

Extended Discussion

Discuss the following questions with a partner. Be prepared to share your answers.

01. What are some reasons that people would choose to only have one child?
02. Is it selfish to have more than two children?
03. Other than a one-child policy, what are some ways to solve the problem of overpopulation?

An International One-Child Policy

Vocabulary and Questions

Take Turns
My sister and I take turns washing the dishes.

Compatibility
My wife and I are really compatible. We have the same hobbies.

Interracial
In the 1960s, interracial marriages were uncommon in America.

Inter-religious
Some countries still ban inter-religious marriages.

Permit
My parents won't permit me to get married until I finish college.

Minimum Wage
It's hard to build a family if you are only earning minimum wage.

Discussion Questions

Discuss the following questions with a partner. Be prepared to share your answers.

01. How do you think cohabitation before marriage will change society?
02. Do you think cohabiting before marriage will make the marriage more likely to succeed?
03. How do you feel about people who spend their lives together, but never get married?
04. Is it okay for your child to live with his/her partner for a year before getting married?
05. If your child still lived at home and wanted his/her partner to come live with you, how would you feel?

Making a Budget

Collaborative Activity

You are a young couple, and you feel like it's too early for you to get married. However, you love each other, and want to live together now. You also want to save money for your future together. Your parents are very traditional, and they don't agree with you living together before marriage, so they refuse to help you financially. This means that you will have to be very careful with your money, so you need to create a monthly budget.

Consider the following:

- The boyfriend has a high school education and works full time.
- He earns 10% more than the local minimum wage per month.
- The girlfriend goes to university and works part-time.
- She earns 70% of the local minimum wage since she works part-time.

Develop a monthly budget for the young couple. Based on the local minimum wage, decide how much they can earn each month. Then, calculate their expenses and how much they can save each month.

Boyfriend's Monthly Income		Girlfriend's Monthly Income	

Rent	Utilities	Insurance	Transportation

Phone	Entertainment	Food	Socializing

Clothing	Miscellaneous	Monthly Savings	

Page 54 — Pros and Cons

Designating Chores

Critical Thinking

You have now been living together for a couple of months. Recently, you have started arguing about the chores. The girlfriend feels like she has a lot to do, because she has to go to university and work a part-time job. She wants the boyfriend to do more chores. The boyfriend feels like he has more to do, because he has a full-time job, and that there is more pressure on him to earn enough money for both of them.

Divide up the chores between the boyfriend and girlfriend.

Consider the following questions:

- *How long does each chore take?*
- *How much energy does each chore take?*
- *Should each chore only be done by one person, or should they take turns?*

01. Washing Dishes   _____

02. Sweeping   _____

03. Mopping   _____

04. Vacuuming   _____

05. Dusting   _____

06. Watering Plants   _____

07. Making the Bed   _____

08. Taking Out the Trash _____

09. Cleaning the Bathroom _____

10. Doing the Laundry   _____

11. Shopping for Groceries _____

12. Cooking   _____

Before and After

Discussion Activity

You have been happily married for 25 years. You have a young friend, and she has decided that she wants to live with her boyfriend. You know that living together with someone is difficult. You decide to give her some advice to increase her chances of success.

Think of five tips that can make it easier to live with someone.

01. _____

02. _____

03. _____

04. _____

05. _____

Discussion Activity

Your young friend has been together with her boyfriend for three years. Unfortunately, it seems they are going to break up. During the three years together, they bought furniture, electronics and a pet. They even have a savings account together. They are arguing over who gets what, and ask for your advice on how to decide.

Think of five points to consider when dividing the property.

01. _____

02. _____

03. _____

04. _____

05. _____

Statistics and Discussion

Cohabitation has increased by nearly 900% over the last 50 years.[2]

In France and Germany, cohabiting couples have a slightly lower risk of divorce.[1]

Check "Statistics Sources" in the back of the workbook for additional information.

Statistics Discussion

Discuss the following questions with a partner.

01. Some statistics suggest that cohabitation leads to a higher divorce rate when couples do get married. Why do you think France and Germany are the exceptions?
02. Why do you think the amount of cohabiting couples has increased by so much so quickly?

Extended Discussion

Discuss the following questions with a partner. Be prepared to share your answers.

01. Do you think cohabitation will replace marriage as the new "normal" way of life?
02. Do you think cohabitation is better for men or for women?
03. Should long-term partners who cohabitate be entitled to the same rights as married couples?

Living Together Before Marriage

Unit 09 — Dating A Colleague

What do you think are the pros and cons of dating a colleague?

Vocabulary and Discussion

Gossip

I don't like when people gossip about me at work.

Company Policy

Since you broke company policy, we will have to let you go.

Break Up

I broke up with my boyfriend because he was cheating on me.

Employee Evaluation

Because of your good employee evaluation, you can get a 10% raise.

Similar

Your daughters look so similar. Are they twins?

Supervisor

My supervisor called me into his office because I was late again.

Discussion Questions

Discuss the following questions with a partner. Be prepared to share your answers.

01. Have you ever dated, or thought about dating, someone you worked with?
02. Do you think gossip would be a big problem for colleagues who are dating?
03. How would your boss react if he/she found out that you were dating a colleague?
04. What if the relationship ended? How would you deal with him/her at work?
05. Do you think it is better to date someone from work, or someone you meet at a bar?

Mat and Jayla

Discussion Activity

Mat and Jayla secretly started dating six months ago, against company policy. Now, their boss has found out that they are together and says that they must stop seeing each other, or one of them will be fired.

Read the following, then choose if they should break up or not. If they stay together, who should leave the company?

Mat works for the company as a salesman. He has been with the company for three years, and earns a basic salary of $3,500USD per month. However, he also earns additional money through commissions. He is a decent employee, and likes his job. His supervisor has said that if he works hard, he might be able to be promoted in a year.

When asked about his relationship with Jayla:

"I really like her a lot, but I am not sure if it is love or not. We have fun together, and I think we might be able to build a future together. If I have to choose between Jayla and my job... well, I guess I would have to choose Jayla."

Jayla works for the company as a marketing supervisor. She has been with the company for five years, and earns a basic salary of $3,000 per month. Due to her position, she has been given a company car to use. She is really good at her job, and enjoys working for the company. Her manager has said that she will probably be promoted again in half a year.

When asked about her relationship with Mat:

"I think I love him, but it has only been six months, so I am not sure. I love my job, and I really don't want to lose it. If I have to choose between my job and Mat, well, I might choose my job. I've worked hard to move up in this company, and I would like to continue moving up."

01.   Should they stay together or break up?   _____

02.   If they break up, who should leave?   _____

Pros and Cons

Company Policy

Collaborative Activity

You work for the HR department in an English school for adults. Some of the employees are dating each other, and some are dating students. Due to the laws in your country, you are not allowed to completely ban employees from dating other adults, so your boss has asked you to create five rules for employee-employee relationships, and five rules for employee-student relationships.

Create rules for employee-employee relationships and employee-student relationships.

Rules for Employee-Employee Relationships

01. _____

02. _____

03. _____

04. _____

05. _____

Rules for Employee-Student Relationships

01. _____

02. _____

03. _____

04. _____

05. _____

Fluency Tip! Sitcoms are a great way to build your listening skills. They are funny, use realistic language and can be saved on your phone to watch when you commute to work. Just remember to turn off the subtitles. The aim is to listen, not to read.

Difficult Choices

Critical Thinking

Read the following situation, then consider each problem. What would you do if you met the same problems? Make a few notes, and then discuss your answers with your partner or group.

Imagine that you got promoted one month ago. However, one week after your promotion, you started dating your boss. You've been dating for three months, but now some other employees have found out about the relationship.

Your colleagues are gossiping that the only reason you got the promotion was because of your "relationship" with your boss. They stop talking to you, and no longer treat you with any respect.

Problem 1: What do you do?
_____
_____
_____
_____

Because of the gossip, you decide to stop dating your boss. Now, an employee evaluation is coming up. A good evaluation from your boss would help your career at the company, but you are afraid your boss will give you a bad evaluation because you broke up with him.

Problem 2: What do you do?
_____
_____
_____
_____

Your boss gave you a bad evaluation. You believe your performance at work was great. If you complain to HR, it may cause a lot of problems for you if you are wrong. However, if you are right and don't complain, you may miss opportunities.

Problem 3: What do you do?
_____
_____
_____
_____

Statistics and Discussion

Almost 70% of people admit to being in an office romance.*

There are four reasons that colleagues date: time, ease, sex and similarity.*

Check "Statistics Sources" in the back of the workbook for additional information.

Statistics Discussion

Discuss the following questions with a partner.

01. The figure of 70% is from the US. Would that number be higher or lower in your country?
02. Which of the four reasons given for dating a colleague would be your reason?
03. Can you think of a fifth reason that a person may date a colleague?

Agree or Disagree

Do you agree or disagree with the following statements?

01. Employees should be allowed to date each other at work.
02. It's impossible to work together after breaking up.
03. If you break up with a colleague, one of you should leave the company.
04. All romantic relationships at work should be reported to the HR department.

Vocabulary and Discussion

Potential

If your wallet is sticking out, it has the potential to be stolen.

Migrate

Ducks and geese migrate during the winter.

Permanent

Immigration means you are moving to a new country permanently.

Risk

There are some risks when moving abroad, but also some rewards.

Adjust

It can be difficult to adjust yourself to the culture of another country.

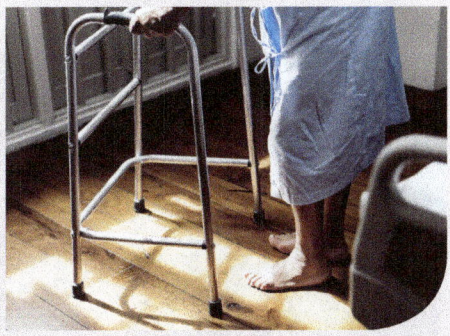

Welfare

Japan has a great welfare system to help senior citizens.

Discussion Questions

Discuss the following questions with a partner. Be prepared to share your answers.

01. Have you ever thought of moving abroad? If so, to where?
02. What would your family say if you decided to move abroad?
03. Do you think you could adjust yourself to the culture of the country you lived in?
04. Is it easier for people to become adjusted to a more developed or less developed countries?
05. Do you think it is easy for people to move to your country?

Qualities to Consider

Discussion Activity

Some countries are safe, while other countries have many job opportunities. Look at the following qualities that people often consider before moving abroad. Which country best represents each quality? For example: Thailand has the best food, because it is fresh, spicy and full of flavor!

Which country best represents each quality and why?

Safety	Job Opportunities	Cost of Living	Cleanliness
Transportation	**Education**	**Public Welfare**	**Green Areas**
Culture	**Entertainment**	**Healthcare**	**Food**

Discussion Activity

Put the 12 qualities in order from most important to least important.

01. _____   05. _____   09. _____

02. _____   06. _____   10. _____

03. _____   07. _____   11. _____

04. _____   08. _____   12. _____

The Top 3

Critical Thinking

According to www.moverdb.com and www.therichest.com, Germany, Russia and the United States are the three countries with the largest number of immigrants.

What are three pros and three cons of moving to each of these three countries?

Germany	Russia	The United States

Pros

01. _____   01. _____   01. _____

02. _____   02. _____   02. _____

03. _____   03. _____   03. _____

Cons

01. _____   01. _____   01. _____

02. _____   02. _____   02. _____

03. _____   03. _____   03. _____

A Care Package

Discussion Activity

Six months ago, you moved abroad. Now, you are really missing the snacks of your country. You contact your family in your hometown, and ask them to send you a care package of the snacks you miss most.

Choose 15 snacks that you would want in the care package.

01. _____
02. _____
03. _____
04. _____
05. _____
06. _____
07. _____
08. _____
09. _____
10. _____
11. _____
12. _____
13. _____
14. _____
15. _____

Statistics and Discussion

About 20% of immigrants are from China, India or the Philippines.*

About half of all immigrants reside in just 10 countries.*

The average age of immigrants from Asia is 33.7.*

Check "Statistics Sources" in the back of the workbook for additional information.

Statistics Discussion

Discuss the following questions with a partner.

01. Why do you think so many people emigrate from China, India and the Philippines?
02. What do you think is the ideal age to immigrate to another country?
03. Which 10 countries do you think are the 10 that attract half of all immigrants?

Agree or Disagree

Do you agree or disagree with the following statements?

01. America is a dangerous country to immigrate to. They have too many guns.
02. People who immigrate are unable to be successful in their own countries.
03. Immigrants take jobs from local people.
04. Local culture is threatened by immigrants.

Moving Abroad

Unit 11 Being Child-free

What do you think are the pros and cons of being child-free?

Vocabulary and Discussion

Calculate

Before having a child, you should calculate how much it will cost.

Daycare

Every morning, I take my son to daycare, and then I go to work.

Charity

The charity gave food and books to the children in the village.

Inheritance

The woman inherited a million dollars when her aunt died.

RV

When I retire, I want to travel the country in a RV.

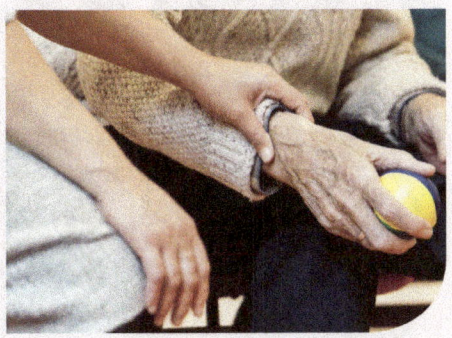

Retirement Community

I'll live in a retirement community when I'm too old to get around.

Discussion Questions

Discuss the following questions with a partner. Be prepared to share your answers.

01. Do you think you could be happy if you chose to never have children?
02. What would you have to give up if you chose to have children?
03. What would you have to give up if you chose to be child-free?
04. What type of person is not suitable to be a parent?
05. Would you worry about your future if you didn't have children?

The Cost of a Child

Collaborative Activity

You and your partner are not sure if you want to have a child or not. You both have middle-income jobs, and you are worried about if you can save enough money for your future if you have a child. You decide to calculate how much it would cost to raise a child until the age of 22.

Calculate how much money you would spend each month on raising a child, and then how much it would cost over 22 years. Remember, costs will change as the child becomes older.

	Average Cost Per Month	Cost Over 22 Years
1. Food		
2. Clothing		
3. Healthcare		
4. Daycare		
5. Social Activities		
6. Entertainment		
7. Education		
8. The Future		
Total Cost		

Pros and Cons

Retirement Plan

Collaborative Activity

You and your spouse have decided to not have children. However, this completely goes against what is common in your culture, and you are worried about what will happen to you when you become older and retire. You have decided to make a retirement plan.

Create a retirement plan by answering the following questions.

01. Where will you live when you retire?

    _____

    _____

02. How much money should you save each month?

    For this question, consider when you plan to retire, and how old you are now. This will determine how much you need to save each month.

    _____

    _____

03. Who will inherit everything when you die?

    _____

    _____

04. What will you do if you partner dies before you?

    _____

    _____

05. Who can help take care of you when you are older?

    _____

    _____

Being Child-free

Difficult Choices

Critical Thinking

Read the following situations, then consider each problem. What would you do if you met the same problems? Make a few notes, and then discuss your answers with your partner or group.

Retirement Activities

You and your partner will retire next year. You both are not sure about what you really want to do when you retire. After much discussion, you are trying to choose between two options:

A. Sell your home and buy a RV. Travel the country and have an adventurous retirement.

B. Sell your home and join a retirement community. It's not very adventurous, but you will have security in the community.

Which do you choose and why?

_____
_____
_____
_____
_____
_____

Inheritance

You made a lot of good choices in life, and now you have a lot of money saved in the bank. However, since you don't have children, there is no one to inherit your money. There are three options you're considering:

A. Leave the money to a friend.

B. Leave the money to the child of a close friend.

C. Donate the money to your favorite charity.

Which do you choose and why?

_____
_____
_____
_____
_____
_____

Use sticky notes to label different items in your home. On the note, write a sentence under the word showing how it is used. This will help you recall new vocabulary, and commit it to your long-term memory.

Page 74 — Pros and Cons

Statistics and Discussion

It takes an average of 8 hours a day to raise a child.*

The average cost to raise a child to the age of 18 in the United States is $200,000.*

20 years of studies have shown that child-free couples are happier than couples with children.*

Check "Statistics Sources" in the back of the workbook for additional information.

Statistics Discussion

Discuss the following questions with a partner.

01. Why do you think it costs so much to raise a child in America?
02. Is it cheaper or more expensive to raise a child in your country?
03. Do you think most parents spend 8 hours a day raising their child?
04. What makes child-free couples happier than couples with children?

Agree or Disagree

Do you agree or disagree with the following statements?

01. Having no children means you will be lonely when you get older.
02. Being child-free means you are selfish, because your parents won't have grandchildren.
03. Being child-free means you'll have much less stress in your life.

Being Child-free

Unit 12 — Cloning

What do you think are the pros and cons of cloning?

Vocabulary and Discussion

Endangered

It's important to protect endangered species, or they'll become extinct.

Extinct

The dinosaurs went extinct about 65 million years ago.

Species

Every year, many species become endangered or extinct.

Deceased

It's lonely when you are old and many of your friends are deceased.

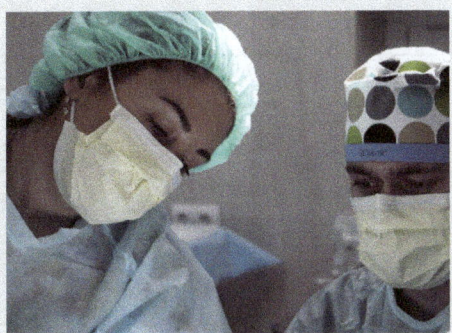

Transplant

The doctor says I won't live much longer without a heart transplant.

Organ

Due to the accident, he suffered damage to several of his organs.

Discussion Questions

Discuss the following questions with a partner. Be prepared to share your answers.

01. Why do you believe so many people are afraid of cloning?
02. Should cloning be used to bring back extinct animals?
03. Do you think cloning meat, not the animal, would be a good way to solve world hunger?
04. Would you eat cloned meat?
05. Which three famous people should be cloned?

Back from Extinction

Discussion Activity

Your laboratory has perfected cloning, and you have the DNA of 15 extinct species. Unfortunately, you only have enough money to clone 5 of the species.

Which five of the following extinct animals do you think need to be cloned, and why?

01.	African Black Rhino	06.	Atlas Bear	11.	Baiji White Dolphin
02.	Saber-toothed Cat	07.	Quagga	12.	Pyrenean Ibex
03.	Woolly Mammoth	08.	Japanese Honshu Wolf	13.	Passenger Pigeon
04.	Irish Elk	09.	Tasmanian Tiger	14.	Steller's Sea Cow
05.	Moa	10.	Caspian Tiger	15.	Pinta Island Tortoise

01. _____

02. _____

03. _____

04. _____

05. _____

Pros and Cons

Organs Inc.

Collaborative Activity

The year is 2035, and organ cloning is now common. You've started an organ production company, and you are looking to earn a profit and grow your business as quickly as possible, but you also want to try to help as many people as you can. You have enough money to begin cloning 10 organs. You need to consider which organs will help the most people, as well as earn you the most money.

Create a list of 10 organs that your company will clone, and how much you'll charge for each.

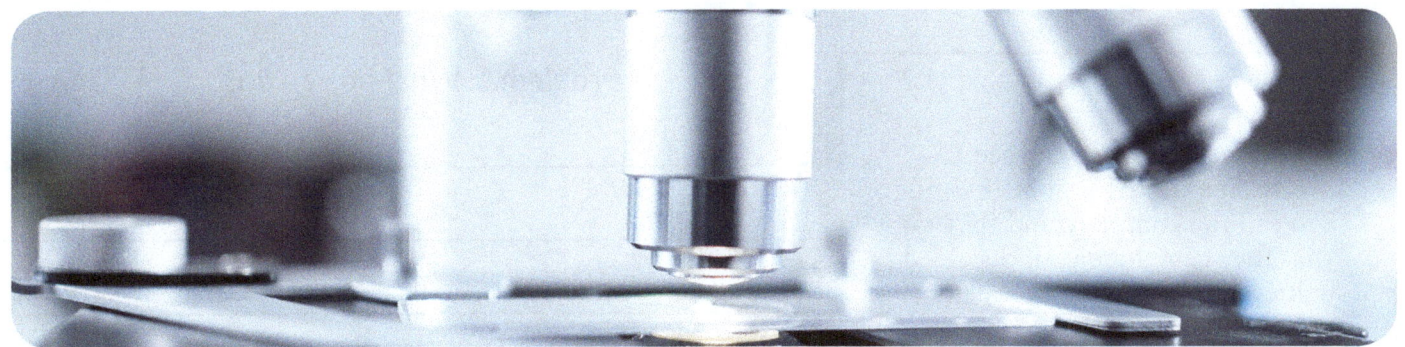

	The Organs	The Prices
01.	_____	_____
02.	_____	_____
03.	_____	_____
04.	_____	_____
05.	_____	_____
06.	_____	_____
07.	_____	_____
08.	_____	_____
09.	_____	_____
10.	_____	_____

Difficult Choices

Critical Thinking

Read the following situation, then consider each problem. What would you do if you met the same problems? Make a few notes, and then discuss your answers with your partner or group.

You got married ten years ago, and had a daughter about five years ago. Your life has been great. Your spouse is wonderful, and your daughter is a joy. You can't imagine a life without either of them. However, one night you are driving home from a cinema, and a drunk driver crashes into your car, and your daughter dies.

Problem 1: What do you do?

It's one year later. You see an advertisement on TV about cloning. You call the company, and they say that they can clone your deceased daughter's body, but not her memories. Your spouse wants to clone her.

Problem 2: What is your choice?

You decide to clone your deceased daughter. When she gets older, will you tell her that she is a clone?

If you decide to tell her, when is the right time to tell her?

Problem 3: What do you do?

You decide to not tell her. Now, she is 15, and she finds out by accident that she is a clone. She is furious with you, and wants to legally separate from you.

Statistics and Discussion

Dolly was the 277th attempt. There were 276 failures before her.*

South Korea was the first in the world to clone a dog in 2005.*

A US law passed in 2008 allows the consumption of cloned meat.*

Check "Statistics Sources" in the back of the workbook for additional information.

Statistics Discussion

Discuss the following questions with a partner.

01. How do you feel about it taking 277 tries to successfully clone a sheep?
02. Why do you think South Korea decided to clone a dog, and not a different animal?
03. Why do you think the US has made a law to allow the consumption of cloned meat, even though it is not yet available?

Extended Discussion

Discuss the following questions with a partner. Be prepared to share your answers.

01. Do you think scientists should be allowed to clone people?
02. What problems could cloning people solve, and what problems could it create?
03. When you are old, would you like to clone your body and transplant your brain into it?

Cloning

Unit 13
Dating During High School

What do you think are the pros and cons of dating during high school?

Vocabulary and Discussion

High School Sweetheart
We've been married for 10 years. We were high school sweethearts.

Freshman
It's exciting to become a high school freshman and start a new journey.

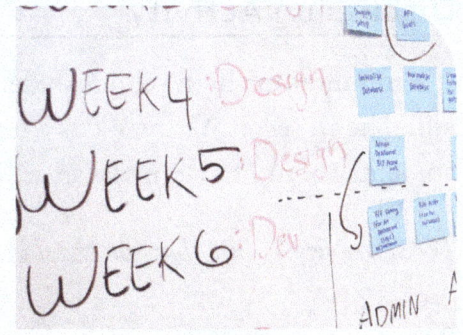

Syllabus
Did you check the class syllabus? It seems we'll have a test next week.

Secret Crush
I had a secret crush in high school. I was too shy to tell her how I felt.

Discourage
My parents discouraged me from dating unless I kept good grades.

Consequence
I had to quit high school as a consequence of becoming pregnant.

Discussion Questions

Discuss the following questions with a partner. Be prepared to share your answers.

01. Do you think students in high school should date, or focus on studying?
02. In high school, did you have a boyfriend or girlfriend? Why or why not?
03. If you were dating, did you tell your parents about it? Do you think your classmates told their parents?
04. Did you have a secret crush in high school? Did you tell him or her?
05. Do you think dating in high school is more or less difficult than dating as an adult?

Tips for Better Choices

Discussion Activity

It's common for high school students to date. Even if parents and teachers tell them not to date, many will still date in secret. You work as a teacher for the local high school, and you think it is important to teach the students about how to make smart choices about dating.

What are five points that you should teach students so that they will make better dating choices?

01. _____

02. _____

03. _____

04. _____

05. _____

 If you understand something, but your partner doesn't, try to explain it to him or her instead of asking the teacher for help. Teaching is the best way to learn something.

Collaborative Activity

You've shared your five points with the principal of the school. She liked your ideas, and has asked you to work with the other teachers to create a new class for the students about dating and future relationships. The class will be for one semester during the students' freshman year.

When designing the new class, consider the following:
- One semester in your school is 3 months.
- The class will be taught once a week.
- Each class will be one hour long.

You should also consider the following questions:
- You need content for 12 classes. What's the topic of each class?
- How will you teach the topic of each class?
- What do you want the students to have learned by the end of each class?

A Class on Dating

Create a new class to teach students about dating, as well as prepare them for future relationships.

Week 01 Topic
Objective

Week 02 Topic
Objective

Week 03 Topic
Objective

Week 04 Topic
Objective

Week 05 Topic
Objective

Week 06 Topic
Objective

Week 07 Topic
Objective

Week 08 Topic
Objective

Week 09 Topic
Objective

Week 10 Topic
Objective

Week 11 Topic
Objective

Week 12 Topic
Objective

Difficult Choices

Critical Thinking

Read the following situation, then consider each problem. What would you do if you met the same problems? Make a few notes, and then discuss your answers with your partner or group.

You are a 16-year-old high school girl. You come from a traditional family, and your parents have said that you are not allowed to date until after you finish high school. So far, that rule has been okay for you, because you haven't been interested in any of the boys at your school.

One week ago, a new student transferred into your class. He sits next to you, and is really nice. You have spoken to him a few times, and you think you like him. He asks you out on a date. You know you are not allowed to date, but you really want to have a try.

Problem 1: What do you do?

You secretly start dating him. You date every weekend for two months. After two months, he asks you to go to a hotel with him.

Problem 2: What do you do?

You went to the hotel with him. Now, it is two months later, and you are pregnant. You are terrified of telling your parents, but you know you will have to tell them.

Problem 3: What do you say to them?

Pros and Cons

Statistics and Discussion

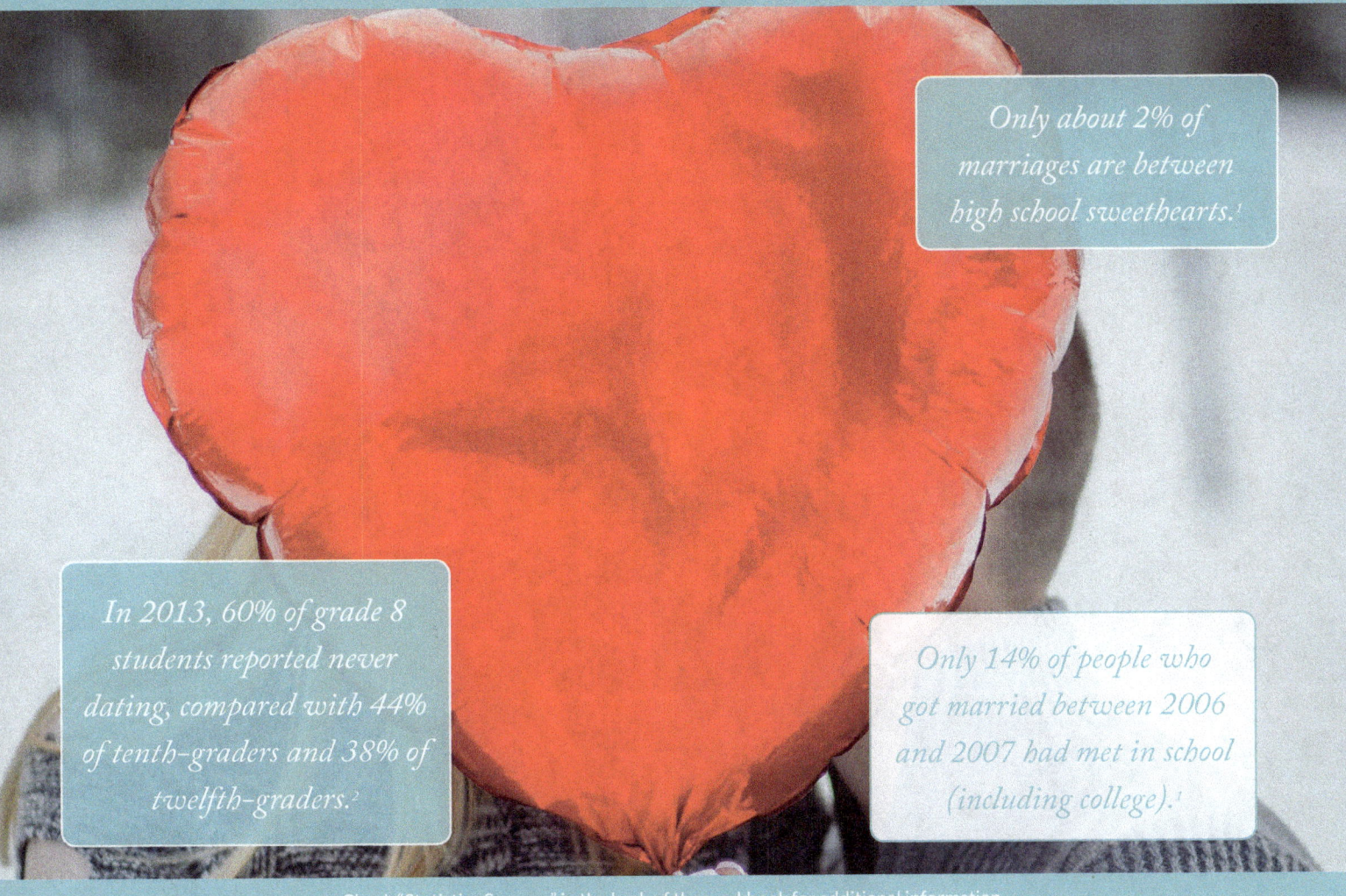

Only about 2% of marriages are between high school sweethearts.[1]

In 2013, 60% of grade 8 students reported never dating, compared with 44% of tenth-graders and 38% of twelfth-graders.[2]

Only 14% of people who got married between 2006 and 2007 had met in school (including college).[1]

Check "Statistics Sources" in the back of the workbook for additional information.

Statistics Discussion

Discuss the following questions with a partner.

01. Is high school dating in your country increasing or decreasing?
02. Since 2013, do you think the numbers of high school dating have gone up or down?
03. Why do you think it is difficult to stay together after school ends?

Agree or Disagree

Do you agree or disagree with the following statements?

01. It's the responsibility of the school to teach kids about relationships.
02. Pregnancy during high school is the fault of the parents.
03. You should talk to your kids about dating as soon as they start middle school.
04. When students focus on studying only, they become book smart, but socially unprepared.

Unit 14
Making Kids Earn Their Allowance

What do you think are the pros and cons of making kids earn their allowance?

Vocabulary and Discussion

Allowance

I give my son an allowance of $10 per week if he does his chores.

Earn

It's important to teach kids to work hard to earn what they want.

Chores

My least favorite chore is mopping the floors. It takes so long!

Invest

Some kids save their allowance to invest in a car when they turn 16.

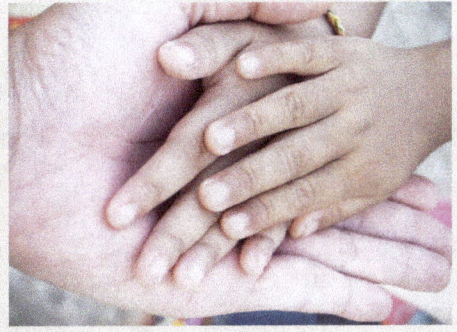

Generation

Kids today are lazy! My generation worked hard to get what we wanted.

Calculate

If I calculated correctly, I saved $5000 last year!

Discussion Questions

Discuss the following questions with a partner. Be prepared to share your answers.

01. What will happen if a child always gets what he or she wants without earning it?
02. What will happen if the child has to work hard to get anything he or she wants?
03. Did your parents make you do a lot of chores as a child? If yes, what were they?
04. Did you earn money as a child, or did your parents just give you what you wanted?
05. Do you think the young generation today is more or less spoiled than your generation?

Earning Money

Discussion Activity

Think of ten chores that a child can do to earn money, and how much the child should earn for each chore.

01. _____ $ _____   06. _____ $ _____

02. _____ $ _____   07. _____ $ _____

03. _____ $ _____   08. _____ $ _____

04. _____ $ _____   09. _____ $ _____

05. _____ $ _____   10. _____ $ _____

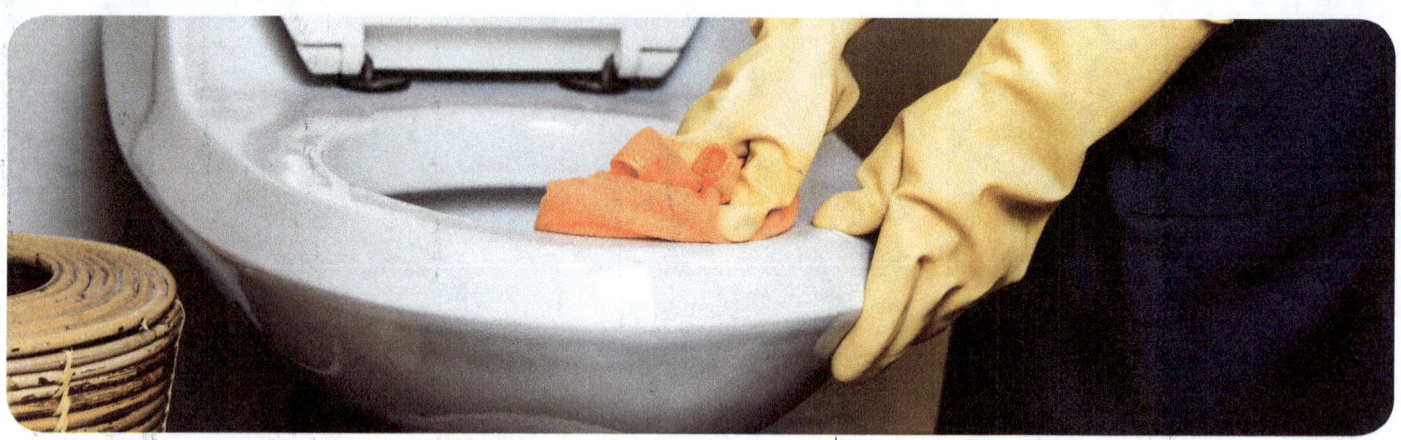

Discussion Activity

Think of five other ways that your child can earn money, and how much the child should earn for each activity. For example, you might give your child $20 for passing a semester at school with high marks.

01. _____ $ _____

02. _____ $ _____

03. _____ $ _____

04. _____ $ _____

05. _____ $ _____

Pros and Cons

Scheduling Chores

Discussion Activity

Your son is 12 years old. You think he is old enough to do more housework. You and your spouse decide to make a list of chores for him to do each day, as well as how much money he can earn each week doing them.

Create a list of chores that your son should do each day, as well as monthly chores he should do.

Monday	Tuesday	Wednesday

Thursday	Friday	Saturday

Sunday	Monthly Chores

Making Kids Earn Their Allowance

Work for It

Collaborative Activity

You are 14 years old, but you are not a normal 14-year-old. You're thinking about your future, and you think it's time that you started a small business after school. You want to be able to take care of yourself and not rely on your parents so much. You decide to save the money you get trough doing chores, and then invest in five items to help you start a business and make more money. You plan to start the business by the time your are 16.

Think about the following points:

- *Consider how much money you could save each month from doing chores.*
- *Decide on a business that you could start as a teenager.*
- *Make a list of the five items you need to buy to start your business.*
- *Decide on the cost of each item.*
- *Decide the order in which you need to purchase the items.*
- *Create a simple business plan for how to start your business.*

How much money can you save each month?

What type of business will you start?

	Item	Cost	Purchase Order
01.	_____	$ _____	_____
02.	_____	$ _____	_____
03.	_____	$ _____	_____
04.	_____	$ _____	_____
05.	_____	$ _____	_____

Your Simple Business Plan

Pros and Cons

Statistics and Discussion

A survey found that 77% of US children have to do chores to earn their allowance.[1]

The average American child makes around $780 per year from his or her allowance. However, only 1% save any of it.[2]

A general rule of thumb is to pay $1 per year of age on a weekly basis. So, if your child is 5, she gets $5 a week. If 12, she gets $12 a week.[2]

Check "Statistics Sources" in the back of the workbook for additional information.

Statistics Discussion

Discuss the following questions with a partner.

01. What percentage of kids in your country do you think earn their money through chores?
02. Do you think $10 for a 10-year-old and $16 for a 16-year-old is fair?
03. How can parents make their children understand the importance of saving money?

Discussing Preferences

Discuss your preferences with your partner. Be prepared to share your answers with the class.

01. Do you prefer paying the bills or shopping for groceries?
02. Do you prefer washing the windows or cleaning the bathroom?
03. Do you prefer washing and drying clothes or ironing?
04. Do you prefer dusting your home and changing the bed linens?

Making Kids Earn Their Allowance

Unit 15 — Banning Smoking

What do you think are the pros and cons of banning smoking?

Vocabulary and Discussion

Ban

Smoking is banned on all flights due to safety concerns.

Public Area

In many countries, people are not allowed to smoke in public areas.

Addiction

It's hard to give up smoking because it can be very addictive.

Campaign

The makeup company launched a campaign promoting a new product.

Peer Pressure

It's hard for young people to say no to peer pressure. They want to fit in.

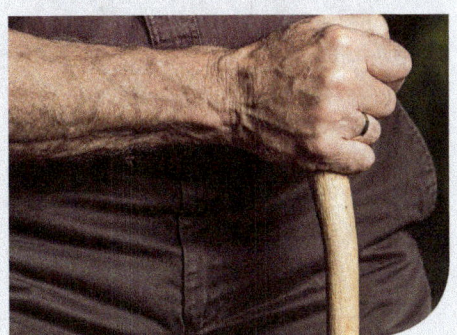

Stroke

My grandfather can't walk well, because he had a stroke last year.

Discussion Questions

Discuss the following questions with a partner. Be prepared to share your answers.

01. Have you, or someone you know, quit smoking?
02. How difficult is it to quit smoking?
03. What are some ways to help people quit smoking?
04. Many people smoke due to stress. What are some healthier ways to deal with stress?
05. Aside from smoking, what are some other things people can become addicted to?

Anti-Smoking Campaign

Discussion Activity

It is very common for young people to start smoking due to peer pressure. Young people feel that if they don't do what their friends are doing, then they won't fit in. Your group has been elected to develop a campaign to help prevent young people from smoking.

Think of five ways to prevent young people from smoking. Consider the following points:

- *What celebrities do kids like in your country?*
- *What media do kids pay attention to?*
- *How do kids speak to each other?*
- *What do kids value in your country?*

01. _____

02. _____

03. _____

04. _____

05. _____

Fading Cigarettes Out

Collaborative Activity

Imagine that smoking is a common problem in your country, with 65% of men smoking, and 30% of women smoking. 1.5 million people in your country die every year from smoking-related illnesses. Your government has decided to ban smoking completely in your country, and has selected your group to create a five-year plan to accomplish this.

Create a five-year plan to fade out and eventually ban smoking.

Year 1

Year 2

Year 3

Year 4

Year 5

Difficult Choices

Critical Thinking

Read the following situation, then consider each problem. What would you do if you met the same problems? Make a few notes, and then discuss your answers with your partner or group.

Imagine that you have a daughter who is 16 years old. Growing up, she was always a good child, but since turning 15, she has become more rebellious. You are worried about her, because you don't want her to get on the wrong track and ruin her life.

One day, you find out that your daughter is dating an 18-year-old boy. He smokes and drinks, and you are worried that he will be a bad influence on her, and that she might even become pregnant and drop out of high school.

Problem 1: What do you do?

You told your daughter to not see the boy anymore, but she didn't listen. She said she was old enough to make her own choices. The next day, you are putting away your daughter's clothes in her room, and you find a pack of cigarettes.

Problem 2: What do you do?

Your daughter admits that she has started smoking, and won't quit. She says it's her life, and she will do what she wants. She has started skipping school and staying out all night.

Problem 3: What do you do?

Statistics and Discussion

Tobacco kills more than 7 million people each year. Around 890,000 of the deaths are from second-hand smoke.[3]

Of the one billion smokers in the world, 80% live in low- and middle-income countries.[2]

There are around 316 million smokers in China, with about 1.5 million Chinese dying every year from related diseases.[1]

Check "Statistics Sources" in the back of the workbook for additional information.

Statistics Discussion

Discuss the following questions with a partner.

01. In China, men typically smoke, but few women do. Why do you think that is?
02. Why do you think most smokers are from low- and middle-income countries?
03. Why do you think some people continue to smoke around friends and family members, even though they know second-hand smoke is harmful?

Extended Discussion

The following are five ways that people use to try to quit smoking. With a partner, put them in order from the most effective to the least effective in your opinion.

_____ 01. Electronic Cigarettes
_____ 02. Stopping Cold Turkey
_____ 03. Meditation or Yoga
_____ 04. Nicotine Gum or Patches
_____ 05. Taking Medication

Banning Smoking

Unit 16: Going Completely Green in 5 Years

What do you think are the pros and cons of your country going completely green within 5 years?

Vocabulary and Discussion

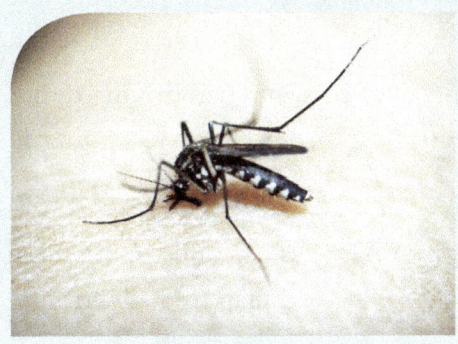

Malaria
Malaria is a dangerous illness that is spread by mosquitoes.

Drought
Because of the long-lasting drought, many animals have left the area.

Infrastructure
The infrastructure of our city needs to be updated to be more efficient.

Relocate
It's hard to pack up and relocate your entire life.

Populace
The populace of the city was pleased with the new open-air market.

Emissions
The emissions from the energy plant have made the air unbreathable.

Discussion Questions

Discuss the following questions with a partner. Be prepared to share your answers.

01. Do you recycle? Are you required to recycle in your country?
02. What are some ways you and your family could be greener?
03. What are some ways you think your company, or school, could be greener?
04. Flying creates a lot of CO_2. Does this mean we should travel less?
05. How long do you think it will take for your country to go completely green?

Driving Greener

Critical Thinking

Your country has decided to ban the production and sell of petrol cars within five years, and ban driving petrol cars within ten years. Instead, all new cars produced and sold must be electric cars. Your country is going to invest heavily in creating an infrastructure to support electric cars.

However, this means that a lot of people will lose money if they just bought a new gas car, and the material waste will be harmful to the environment. Your government has selected you to create a plan to deal with the problems and create a smooth transition.

Solve the following problems.

What program will you create to help prevent citizens from losing money?	
What will you do to get citizens to support the program?	
What will you do with all of the gas cars that are still functional?	
What will you do with the tires from the gas cars that are not functional?	
What will you do with the metal from the gas cars that are not functional?	
How else will you reuse other parts from gas cars that are not functional?	

Relocating the Populace

Collaborative Activity

Imagine that the most populated city in your country is located next to the ocean. Due to climate change, the ocean is rising, and the top scientists in your country have said that the city will be wiped out within five years.

Create a plan to relocate the population of the city to three other areas within your country.

Consider the following questions:
- *Which areas will be able to provide job opportunities for the incoming people?*
- *Should you divide people based on skills? If so, how?*
- *Should you divide people based on age? If so, how?*
- *How will the incoming people impact the local economies?*
- *How will the incoming people impact the local cultures?*

Area 1	Area 2	Area 3
Which three areas will you choose and why?		
Which groups of people will you send to each area and why?		
How will the economy of each area be impacted?		
How will the cultures of each area be impacted?		

Into the Future

Discussion Activity

How will each of the following change in 50 years due to climate change?

Transportation	Homes	Clothing

Technology	Weather	Healthcare

Insurance	Education	Leisure Activities

FLUENCY TIP! When you learn new vocabulary and phrases, consider how you can relate them to yourself. If you can apply them to your life, then you will be more likely to use and retain them.

Pros and Cons

Statistics and Discussion

In the last 130 years, the world has warmed by approximately .85°C.[2]

As of 2019, China is the largest producer of CO$_2$ emissions in the world.[1]

Between 2030 and 2050, climate change is expected to cause approximately 250,000 additional deaths per year.[2]

Check "Statistics Sources" in the back of the workbook for additional information.

Statistics Discussion

Discuss the following questions with a partner.

01. Is it fair to force developing countries to be environmentally friendly as they develop?
02. Do you think the increase in temperature is really man-made, or is it natural?
03. How do you think climate change will contribute to additional deaths each year?

Agree or Disagree

Do you agree or disagree with the following statements?

01. Climate change can be reversed if we invest enough money in green technologies.
02. Your country is doing enough to combat climate change.
03. Climate change is part of the Earth's natural cycle.

Going Completely Green in 5 Years

Unit 17
Nuclear Weapons and Energy

What do you think are the pros and cons of eliminating nuclear weapons and energy?

Vocabulary and Discussion

Arsenal

The military has an arsenal of guns, swords and cannons.

Power Plant

The local power plant generates all of the electricity for the state!

Meltdown

The sea around the nuclear plant was poisoned by its meltdown.

Evacuate

Firemen helped the people to evacuate the burning building.

Retaliate

I left Sue, and she retaliated by breaking my windshield.

Launch

It's amazing to watch a space shuttle launch into space.

Discussion Questions

Discuss the following questions with a partner. Be prepared to share your answers.

01. How do you think the people who created nuclear bombs felt ten years after WWII?
02. Do you think WWII could have been won without the use of nuclear weapons?
03. Do you believe humans are responsible enough to have nuclear weapons?
04. Do you believe nuclear power plants are safe?
05. Are there any better options other than nuclear power plants?

Terms and Conditions

Collaborative Activity

Your group represents your country in an international talk for nuclear disarmament with countries from around the world. However, you are afraid that if you agree to disarm and destroy all of your nuclear weapons, other countries might secretly keep some of their nuclear arsenal.

Decide on 10 conditions that other countries must agree to in order for you to disarm.

01. _____

02. _____

03. _____

04. _____

05. _____

06. _____

07. _____

08. _____

09. _____

10. _____

A New Plant Site

Discussion Activity

During a recent earthquake, a nuclear power plant in your country was damaged and had a meltdown. The surrounding town had to be evacuated. After this disaster, your country's government has elected you to choose a new, ideal location for a nuclear power plant in your country.

Make a list of 10 points to consider when choosing a new place to build a nuclear power plant. After creating your list, choose which location(s) in your country would be ideal for a new nuclear power plant.

01. _____

02. _____

03. _____

04. _____

05. _____

06. _____

07. _____

08. _____

09. _____

10. _____

Which location(s) in your country do you think are the most ideal for a new nuclear power plant, and why?

_____

_____

_____

Nuclear Waste Disposal

Critical Thinking

Your country has several nuclear power plants. So far, they have been keeping their waste near them, but the amount of waste is growing too large. Your government has decided it is time to find a permanent place to bury nuclear waste.

Decide on which three locations in your country are the most ideal for housing nuclear waste in an underground facility, and explain why.

01. _____

_____

_____

02. _____

_____

_____

03. _____

_____

_____

Statistics and Discussion

The US spent $5.8 trillion on nuclear weapons between the early 1940s and 1996.

Just 50 nuclear bombs could kill 200 million people.

Latin America, the South Pacific and Southeast Asia have all agreed to not have nuclear weapons.

Check "Statistics Sources" in the back of the workbook for additional information.

Statistics Discussion

Discuss the following questions with a partner.

01. Why do you think the three areas in the white box agreed to not have nuclear weapons?
02. Why do you think the US invests so heavily in its nuclear arsenal?
03. Which country do you think invests the most in nuclear weapons after the US?

Extended Discussion

Discuss the following questions with a partner.

01. Would you live near a nuclear power plant if you could pay less for electricity?
02. Would you rather live near a nuclear power plant or a coal power plant?
03. Would you work at a nuclear power plant if the salary was good?
04. Are there any countries that shouldn't be allowed to have nuclear power plants?

Unit 18: Open International Immigration

What do you think are the pros and cons of allowing open international immigration?

Vocabulary and Discussion

Immigrate

I immigrated to the US in 2006 for more opportunities.

Emigrate

I emigrated from my country because I wanted a new life.

Fade Away

As populations become more diverse, local cultures may fade away.

Populate

After creating a new pond, the park had to populate it with fish.

Recipient

I won the contest and was the recipient of a brand new car!

Asylum

There is a war in my country, so I am seeking asylum in Germany.

Discussion Questions

Discuss the following questions with a partner. Be prepared to share your answers.

01. Which country do you think most people want to immigrate to?
02. Which country do you think most people want to emigrate from?
03. If immigration is open, how can you protect jobs within your country?
04. Are you concerned that open immigration may make some cultures fade away?
05. How do you think open, international immigration would influence the English language?

Population Loss and Gain

Discussion Activity

Every year, people are leaving their homes to move abroad in search of a new life. Some countries lose population to emigration, while others gain in population through immigration. With your partner, discuss why you think each of the following countries either lose or gain population through immigration.

Why do you think each of these countries are attractive to immigrants?

Australia
Canada
Russia
Germany
Chile
South Africa
The United States

Put the countries in order from which gains the most number of immigrants to which gains the least. Be prepared to explain your reasons.

01. _____   05. _____
02. _____   06. _____
03. _____   07. _____
04. _____

Put the countries in order from which loses the most number of people to emigration to which loses the least. Be prepared to explain your reasons.

01. _____   05. _____
02. _____   06. _____
03. _____   07. _____
04. _____

Why do you think each of these countries lose population to emigration each year?

Greenland
China
South Korea
Mexico
India
Ukraine
Egypt

Populating a New Country

Collaborative Activity

Imagine that you have created a new country. Other countries have agreed to send people to help populate your new country. You have decided to accept people from 12 different countries to populate your new country. You want to choose people who will help establish a positive culture, technological foundation, cuisine, etc.

Make a list of 12 countries that you will receive people from to populate your new country, and what percentage of your population will each country's people make up. In addition, explain your reasons.

Example

Country	Percentage	Reason
Japan	15%	I think it would make the culture more polite.

	Country	Percentage	Reason
01.		%	
02.		%	
03.		%	
04.		%	
05.		%	
06.		%	
07.		%	
08.		%	
09.		%	
10.		%	
11.		%	
12.		%	

Open International Immigration

The Connected World

Critical Thinking

France limits the amount of English music played on radio stations at certain times, because they want to keep their language pure. Come up with ten ways that a country can keep it's unique culture in a connected world.

01. _____

02. _____

03. _____

04. _____

05. _____

06. _____

07. _____

08. _____

09. _____

10. _____

Statistics and Discussion

In 2015, the number of immigrants worldwide was the highest ever recorded, having reached 244 million.*

Close to 1 in 5 migrants in the world live in the top 20 largest cities.*

In 2015, Germany became the largest single recipient of first-time individual asylum claims globally.*

Check "Statistics Sources" in the back of the workbook for additional information.

Statistics Discussion

Discuss the following questions with a partner.

01. Why do you think immigrants are attracted to larger cities?
02. Why do you think Germany chose to open its doors to people seeking asylum?
03. Do you think more countries should follow Germany's example?

Agree or Disagree

Do you agree or disagree with the following statements?

01. Immigrants take jobs from local people.
02. Local cultures are lost due to immigration.
03. Immigrants don't integrate with the locals.
04. More immigration means more crime.

Unit 19: Marrying Outside of Your Culture

What do you think are the pros and cons of marrying someone from another culture?

Vocabulary and Discussion

Merge

As the two countries traded more, their cultures began to merge.

To Wed

We've been together for 3 years, and will wed next month.

Native

I am a native of Thailand, but I currently live in Canada.

Compromise

I didn't want a child, but my wife did. We compromised and got a cat.

Negative

The hotel room was dirty, so I gave it a negative review online.

Positive

A loving family will have a positive impact on a child's development.

Discussion Questions

Discuss the following questions with a partner. Be prepared to share your answers.

01. Would you consider marrying someone from another country?
02. What do you think is most important when choosing someone to wed?
03. Some people believe that interracial babies are more beautiful. Do you think this is true?
04. Would your family support you if you married someone from outside of your culture?
05. Would you be supportive of your child if he or she decided to marry someone from another culture?

Traditions and Compromise

Discussion Activity

Every country and culture has customs that may be difficult for people from other countries and cultures to accept. Make a list of ten customs or family traditions in your culture that people from another culture might have trouble accepting or understanding.

Example

> In Chinese culture, it is common to live with the husband's parents. In countries where parents and children live apart, this might be a hard custom to accept for some people.

01. _____
02. _____
03. _____
04. _____
05. _____
06. _____
07. _____
08. _____
09. _____
10. _____

With a partner, discuss possible ways to compromise on each of the customs and family traditions you listed.

Example

> Instead of living with the husband's parents, they could rent an apartment nearby so that they could spend more time together, or stay with the husband's parents on the weekends.

Pros and Cons

Blending Cultures

Collaborative Activity

As the world becomes more connected, cultures are changing faster than ever. When cultures merge, it is common for a something negative in a culture to be replaced by something positive from another culture. Think of five negatives in your culture, and replace each negative with a positive from another culture.

Example

> Students here are often shy and quiet in class, so they can't improve their English, because they don't speak enough. I'd like them to be more outgoing in class, like students in Mexico.

Something Negative from Your Culture | **Something Positive from Another Culture**

Marrying Outside of Your Culture

Difficult Choices

Critical Thinking

Read the following situation, then consider each problem. What would you do if you met the same problems? Make a few notes, and then discuss your answers with your partner or group.

Imagine that you are from the United Kingdom, and your husband comes from a parents-first culture. This has never been a problem before, but now you are pregnant, and it looks like things are starting to change.

You give birth to a daughter. Your in-laws want you to raise her in their country. Your husband agrees, and he is pushing you to move back to his country. However, you don't think this is best for your child.

Problem 1: What do you do?

You convince your husband that staying in the UK is best, and now the in-laws want to move to the UK to help raise the child. They are very traditional, and think a woman's place is at home. You are concerned about how this might impact your daughter's development.

Problem 2: What do you do?

They move to the UK. Your mother-in-law is very critical of how you are raising your daughter, and often contradicts you, and teaches your daughter things you don't agree with. Your husband supports her and not you.

Problem 3: What do you do?

Pros and Cons

Statistics and Discussion

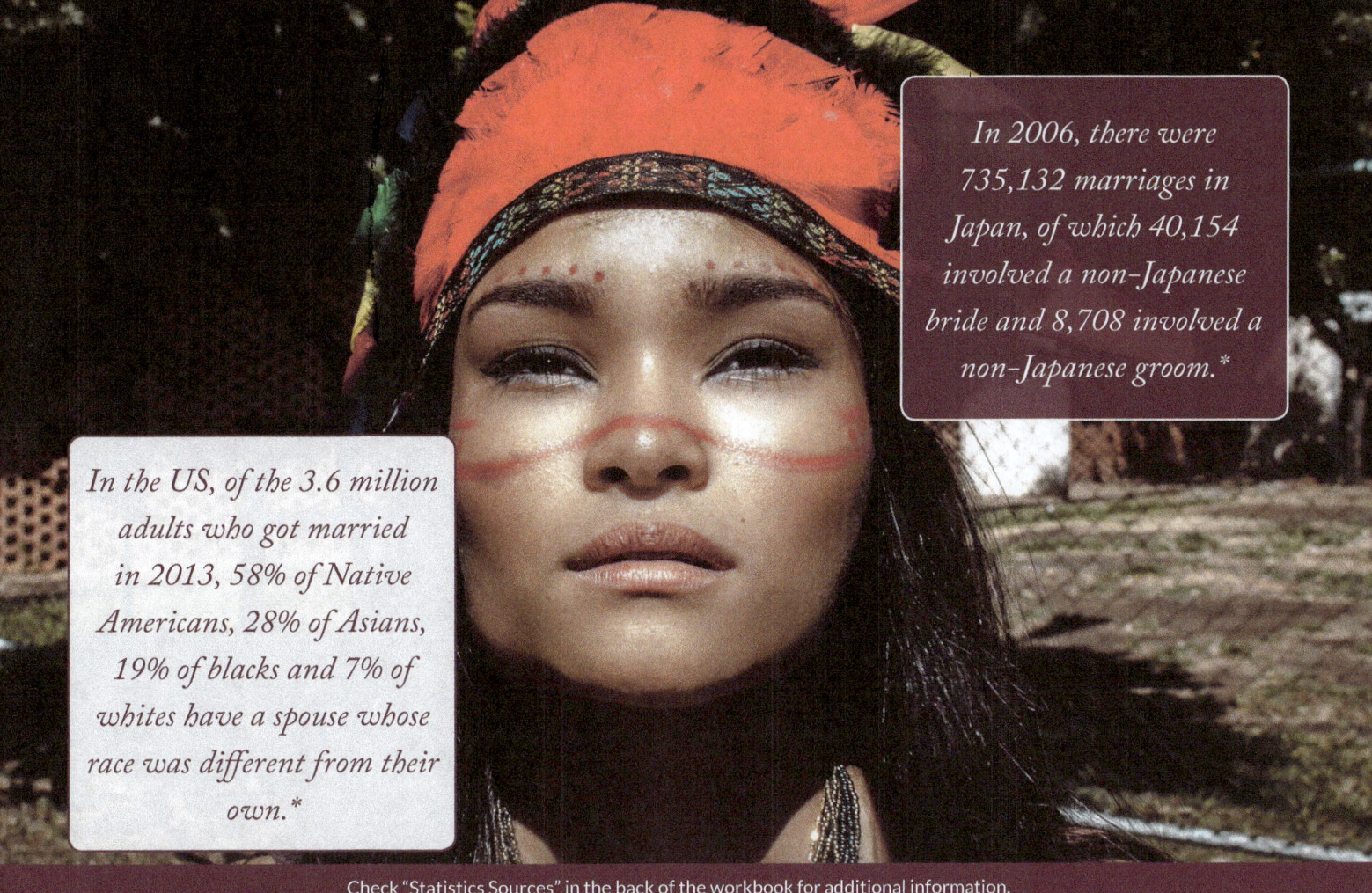

In 2006, there were 735,132 marriages in Japan, of which 40,154 involved a non-Japanese bride and 8,708 involved a non-Japanese groom.*

In the US, of the 3.6 million adults who got married in 2013, 58% of Native Americans, 28% of Asians, 19% of blacks and 7% of whites have a spouse whose race was different from their own.*

Check "Statistics Sources" in the back of the workbook for additional information.

Statistics Discussion

Discuss the following questions with a partner.

01. Why do you think Native Americans are more likely to marry someone from another race?
02. Why do you think white people in the US are the least likely to marry outside their race?
03. Why do Japanese men tend to marry foreigners more than Japanese women?

Extended Discussion

Discuss the following questions with a partner.

01. Which country's culture do you think would be the easiest/hardest for you to adjust to?
02. Do you think there are any country's that have "harmful" cultures?
03. Other than your country's culture, if the world could only have one culture, which country's culture would you want it to be?

Unit 20: Harsher Punishments

What do you think are the pros and cons of harsher punishments for criminals?

Vocabulary and Discussion

Minor Crime

Shoplifting is only a minor crime, but he went to prison for five years!

Major Crime

I think the punishments for major crimes, like murder, should be severe.

Fine

I was speeding, so I had to pay a $200 fine.

Harsh

The punishment was too harsh! A year in prison for stealing a camera?

Incarceration

America has the highest incarceration rate in the world.

Homicide

A homicide detective's job is to investigate murders.

Discussion Questions

Discuss the following questions with a partner. Be prepared to share your answers.

01. Do you believe citizens should be allowed to also punish people who break the law?
02. How can citizens punish law-breakers?
03. How often do you think the legal system makes a mistake?
04. If it is found that an innocent person was put into prison, what should be done?
05. Are there some things in your country that are illegal that you think should be legal?

Local Crimes

Discussion Activity

Make a list of ten minor and major crimes in your country, and how they are usually punished.

Example

Crossing the street when the light is red. $100 fine

The Crime   The Punishment

01. _____   _____
02. _____   _____
03. _____   _____
04. _____   _____
05. _____   _____
06. _____   _____
07. _____   _____
08. _____   _____
09. _____   _____
10. _____   _____

Do you think each punishment is too harsh, or not harsh enough?

Example

I don't think $100 is enough. I think we should double it, or send them to jail for a couple of days. Crossing the street when the light is red endangers other people!

The Punishments

Critical Thinking

Many people believe that punishments need to be very harsh to make people afraid of breaking the law. Without harsh punishments, many people may not care if they get caught. What you think is the appropriate punishment for each crime?

Littering	Speeding	Driving Under the Influence

Shoplifting	Rape	Arson

Kidnapping	Blackmail	Assault

Hit and Run	1st Degree Murder	Manslaughter

Gun-Control

Collaborative Activity

For more than 200 years, the citizens of your country have had the right to have guns. This wasn't a problem long ago, but now guns have become a lot more dangerous, and gun violence is on the rise in your country. Your government has chosen you to create new gun-control laws, but says that you cannot ban guns completely.

Answer the following questions.

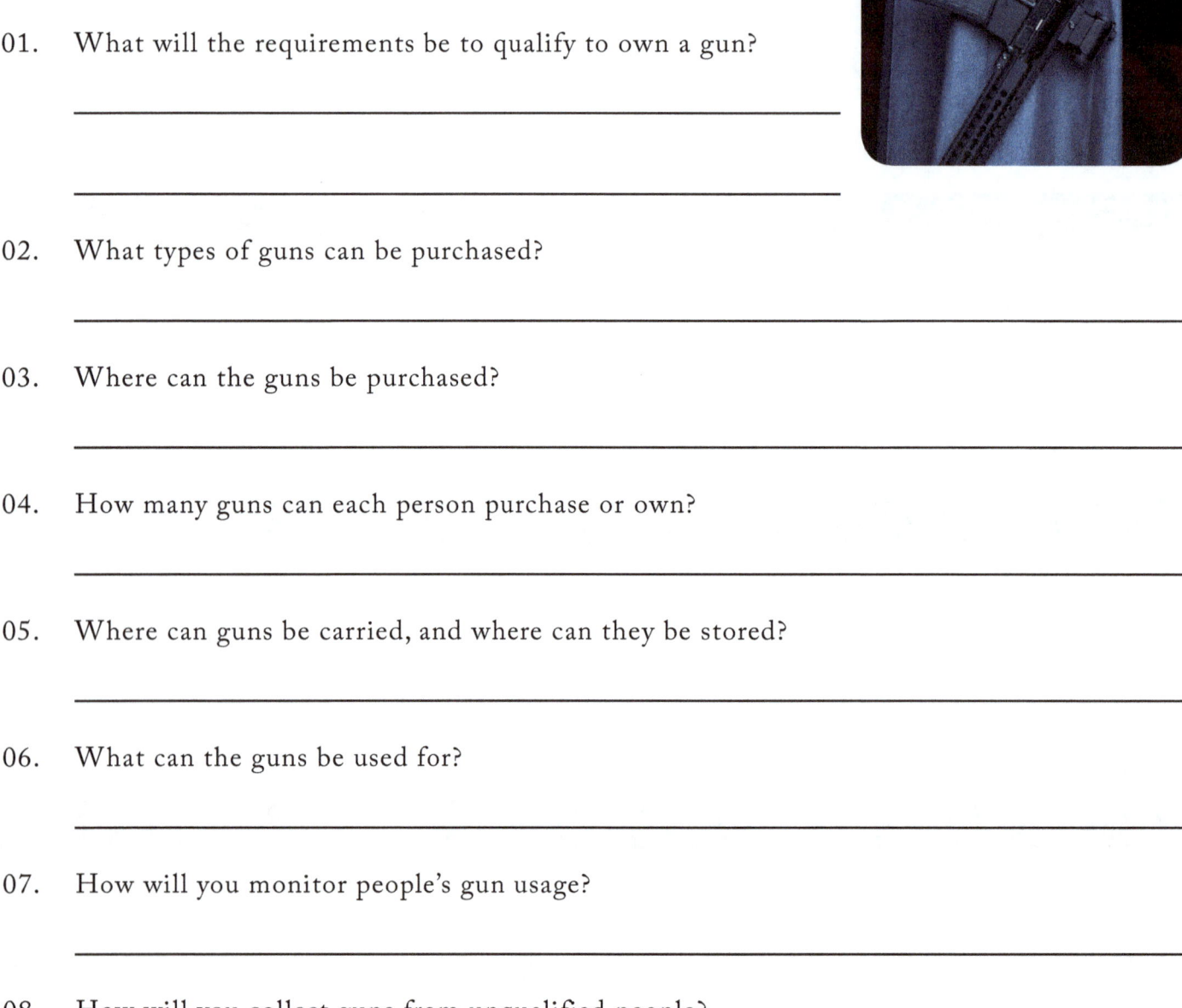

01. What will the requirements be to qualify to own a gun?
    _____
    _____

02. What types of guns can be purchased?
    _____

03. Where can the guns be purchased?
    _____

04. How many guns can each person purchase or own?
    _____

05. Where can guns be carried, and where can they be stored?
    _____

06. What can the guns be used for?
    _____

07. How will you monitor people's gun usage?
    _____

08. How will you collect guns from unqualified people?
    _____

Statistics and Discussion

The United States has the highest incarceration rate in the world. Out of every 100,000 people, 665 are in prison.[2]

El Salvador has the highest murder rate in the world. According to statistics, an average of 82.84, out of 100,000 people, are murdered.[1]

Check "Statistics Sources" in the back of the workbook for additional information.

Statistics Discussion

Discuss the following questions with a partner.

01. Which country do you think has the lowest murder rate?
02. Why do you think the United States has such a high incarceration rate?

Extended Discussion

Discuss the following questions with a partner.

01. Is it more important to punish or rehabilitate criminals?
02. Do you think your country does enough to fight crime?
03. What do you think is the best way for a country to reduce crime?
04. Do you think the punishments for rich people and poor people are equal?

Unit 21 — Dating Students

What do you think are the pros and cons of dating a student?

Vocabulary and Discussion

Passion

Passion is important in a relationship, but it doesn't last long.

Be Attracted To

The mouse was attracted to the cheese in the trap.

Policy

HR asked me to sign a form agreeing to the new working policy.

Semester

A semester at school is usually three months.

Graduate

After I graduate from university, I can finally be a doctor!

Threaten

He threatened to hit me if I didn't stop dating his daughter.

Discussion Questions

Discuss the following questions with a partner. Be prepared to share your answers.

01. Have you ever been attracted to one of your teachers?
02. Would you ever date, seriously or not, one of your teachers?
03. What are the differences between dating a teacher who teaches your class, and dating a teacher who doesn't teach your class?
04. How is dating in a language training school, university and high school different?
05. How would you feel if you child was dating his or her teacher?

In University

Critical Thinking

Imagine that you work as a professor in a university. For each situation, decide on two choices you could make, and what is a possible consequence of each choice. Then, decide which choice you would choose.

One of the students in the university wants to date you. She is 21, and she is not in any of your classes.

Choice A	Choice B

Possible Consequence	Possible Consequence

You decide to date her. During the next semester, she becomes a student in one of your classes. This is against university policy.

Choice A	Choice B

Possible Consequence	Possible Consequence

You continue to date her in secret. The university finds out six months later, and threatens to fire you if you don't end the relationship, but you really like her. It's your job or her.

Choice A	Choice B

Possible Consequence	Possible Consequence

Pros and Cons

In High School

Discussion Activity

You are a high school teacher. You know one of your students is attracted to you. She wants to go to your apartment. She is 18, and will graduate in four months.

Make a list of short-term consequences to the teacher and the student.

Consequences for the Teacher	Consequences for the Student
01. _____	01. _____
02. _____	02. _____
03. _____	03. _____
04. _____	04. _____
05. _____	05. _____

Make a list long-term consequences to the teacher and the student.

Consequences for the Teacher	Consequences for the Student
01. _____	01. _____
02. _____	02. _____
03. _____	03. _____
04. _____	04. _____
05. _____	05. _____

Discussion Question

Despite all of the possible consequences, you decide to date her. You really enjoy spending time with her, and begin to think about building a future with her. However, her parents find out, and threaten to report you to the high school if you don't break up. What do you do?

Dating Students

In a Language School

Collaborative Activity

You are going to open a language training school for adults. Due to local laws, you are not allowed to ban your teachers from dating the students, but you can create some rules to protect the school, students and teachers.

Make a list of ten rules that teachers must follow if they date students, and what are the consequences of breaking each rule.

> **Example**
> The teacher must report the relationship to HR. If the teacher doesn't, the teacher will pay a penalty fee.

Rule 01: _____

Rule 02: _____

Rule 03: _____

Rule 04: _____

Rule 05: _____

Rule 06: _____

Rule 07: _____

Rule 08: _____

Rule 09: _____

Rule 10: _____

FLUENCY TIP! Quality is more important than quantity. Instead of trying to memorize 20 words a day, it may be better to try to memorize five. That way, you can focus on using those five words all day, and be more likely to remember them.

Statistics and Discussion

In the United States, one survey that was conducted with psychology students reported that 10% had sexual interactions with their educators.*

Check "Statistics Sources" in the back of the workbook for additional information.

Statistics Discussion

Discuss the following question with a partner.

This statistic was reported by psychology students. Think of three other majors. What do you think the statistic for those majors would be?

_____

_____

_____

Extended Discussion

Discuss the following questions with a partner.

01. What should the punishment be for a high school teacher who dates a student who is not in his or her class?
02. What should the punishment be if a university teacher dates a student from another class?
03. Should there be any rules about dating adults who are your students in training schools?

Dating Students — Page 135

Unit 22 — Being Your Own Boss

What do you think are the pros and cons of being your own boss?

Vocabulary and Discussion

Entrepreneur
The man wanted to open his own business and be an entrepreneur.

March
The band marched down the street during the city's parade.

Start-up
Jack agreed to invest time and money in Susan's new start-up.

Sacrifice
Sometimes, you have to sacrifice one piece to win the game.

Savings
After paying all of my bills, I didn't have any savings left.

Scale a Business
My start-up has done well. I think it is time to scale it and expand.

Discussion Questions

Discuss the following questions with a partner. Be prepared to share your answers.

01. What do you think it means to 'be your own boss'?
02. What's the most difficult aspect of working for other people?
03. What's the most rewarding aspect of working for yourself?
04. Do you know anyone who started their own business, but was unsuccessful?
05. Do you think you have what it takes to be an entrepreneur?

Skills and Considerations

Discussion Activity

What are ten skills that a person should have to be a successful entrepreneur?

01. _____ 06. _____

02. _____ 07. _____

03. _____ 08. _____

04. _____ 09. _____

05. _____ 10. _____

Compare your list with a partner. What do you agree on, and what do you disagree on?

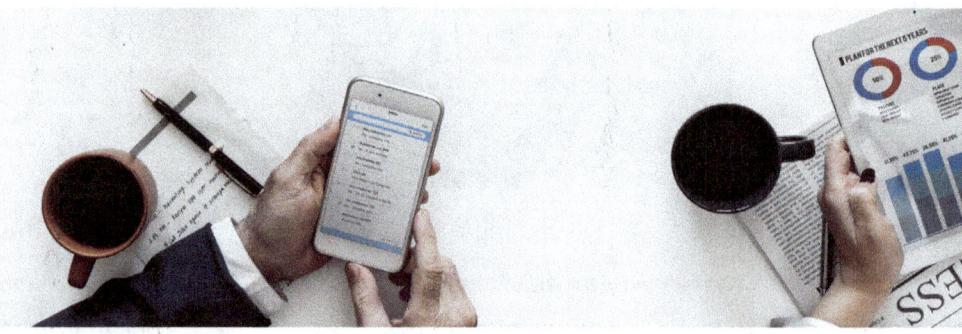

What are ten things you should consider before starting a business?

01. _____ 06. _____

02. _____ 07. _____

03. _____ 08. _____

04. _____ 09. _____

05. _____ 10. _____

Compare your list with a partner. What do you agree on, and what do you disagree on?

Pros and Cons

Being Prepared

Discussion Activity

An entrepreneur will face many challenges, so you should be prepared for the worst before starting your business, or else your business may be doomed to fail before it starts.

Make a list of ten problems you might encounter when opening and running your new business.	*What do you think is the solution for each of the problems you listed?*
01. _____	01. _____
02. _____	02. _____
03. _____	03. _____
04. _____	04. _____
05. _____	05. _____
06. _____	06. _____
07. _____	07. _____
08. _____	08. _____
09. _____	09. _____
10. _____	10. _____

Being Your Own Boss

Difficult Choices

Critical Thinking Activity

Read the following situation, then consider each problem. What would you do if you met the same problems? Make a few notes, and then discuss your answers with your partner or group.

You've finally done it! You've finally saved up enough money to start your own business, and you are incredibly excited! Not only that, but you just got married to the woman of your dreams, and have even started talking about having a family together. Life is looking good, and you are ready to live the perfect life.

You started your own business six months ago. Sadly, it isn't doing well, and your are losing money. You have enough money for three more months.

Problem 1: What do you do?
_____
_____
_____
_____
_____

You worked harder, and you managed to save your business. However, your spouse is upset that you are never home. It's the business or your marriage.

Problem 2: What do you do?
_____
_____
_____
_____
_____

You try to balance your business and home life, but you fail, and your wife leaves you. One year later, your business fails. You have no marriage, no savings, and your home gets taken by the bank.

Problem 3: What do you do?
_____
_____
_____
_____
_____

Statistics and Discussion

*Scaling too fast and too soon is the number one reason most new companies fail.**

*Two founders, rather than one, significantly increases your odds of success. You will raise 30% more investment, grow your customers three times as fast, and will be less likely to scale too fast.**

Check "Statistics Sources" in the back of the workbook for additional information.

Statistics Discussion

Discuss the following questions with a partner.

01. Who would you trust to be a co-founder of your new business?
02. Why do you think "scaling too fast and too soon" causes so many new businesses to fail?

Extended Discussion

What are three ways that you can set-up a new company so that it will be able to scale smoothly as it grows?

01. _____

02. _____

03. _____

Unit 23 — Divorce

What do you think are the pros and cons of divorce?

Vocabulary and Discussion

Separate

Before divorcing, my wife and I decided to separate for a few months.

Upwards Trend

Divorce rates in my country are on an upwards trend.

Equality

The company treated all employees with equality and fairness.

Infidelity

My infidelity with her best friend made my wife decide to leave me.

Abuse

Physical abuse is a common cause of divorce in many countries.

Intimacy

Intimacy is an important part of a romantic relationship.

Discussion Questions

Discuss the following questions with a partner. Be prepared to share your answers.

01. How do you feel about divorce?
02. When do you think divorce can be a good thing?
03. When people divorce, should the property always be divided equally?
04. Some people worry that divorce can have a negative impact on children. Do you think this is true?
05. What would make you decide to get a divorce?

Reasons for Divorce

Discussion Activity

What do you think are the most common reasons for divorce?

01. _____
02. _____
03. _____
04. _____
05. _____
06. _____
07. _____
08. _____
09. _____
10. _____

Compare your list with a partner or group. What's missing?

Work with your partner or group. Choose five reasons from your list. What can be done to reduce the rate of divorce caused by each of the five items?

01. _____
02. _____
03. _____
04. _____
05. _____

A Marriage Course

Collaborative Activity

You work at the local counseling center in your city. You want to attract more business to your center by designing an eight-class course for people who plan to get married. The purpose of the course is to help marriages have a better chance of success.

Consider the following points:
- What is the topic of each class?
- What methods will you use to teach each topic?
- Will you give examples?
- What skills will you teach?

Example
Topic: Abuse

We will teach through conversation and show video examples of victims of abuse.

We will teach anger management and conversation skills.

Week 1

Week 2

Week 3

Week 4

Week 5

Week 6

Week 7

Week 8

Minimizing the Impact

Collaborative Activity

You have decided to get a divorce. However, you have two children, and you are worried about how the divorce may impact the children. The youngest, a girl, is 5. The oldest, a boy, is 13.

How should you explain the divorce to the youngest child?

_____

_____

How should you explain the divorce to the oldest child?

_____

_____

What are five ways that you can reduce the negative impact of the divorce on them?

01. _____
02. _____
03. _____
04. _____
05. _____

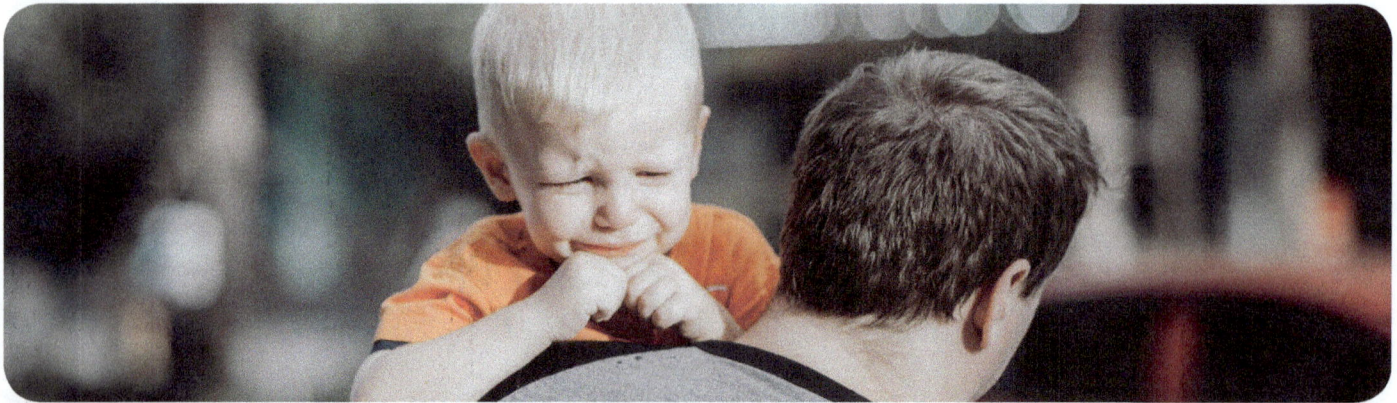

Page 146 — Pros and Cons

Statistics and Discussion

Some statistics show that people who get married later in life are far less likely to divorce.[1]

Since 2000, many countries have shown a decline in divorce.[2]

Check "Statistics Sources" in the back of the workbook for additional information.

Statistics Discussion

Discuss the following questions with a partner.

01. Why do you think people who get married later in life are less likely to divorce?
02. Why do you think the rate of divorce is on the decline in many countries?

Agree or Disagree

Do you agree or disagree with the following statements?

01. A rising divorce rate is a good sign of a society's development.
02. A rising divorce rate shows women are becoming more equal in a society.
03. The law should require people to separate for six months before allowing a divorce.
04. People shouldn't be allowed to wed until after they turn 30.

Unit 24 — Dating Apps

What do you think are the pros and cons of dating apps?

Vocabulary and Discussion

Chemistry

We enjoy spending time together, because we have good chemistry.

Match

We are a good match, because we help each other be better people.

Premium

I pay each month to be a premium member and get more matches.

Profile

When you join Facebook, you have to fill out your profile.

Tap/Swipe

If you like someone, tap the heart or swipe right.

Filter

A filter keeps what you don't want separate from what you do want.

Discussion Questions

Discuss the following questions with a partner. Be prepared to share your answers.

01. Do you use, or have you ever used, a dating app?
02. Which dating app is the most popular in your country?
03. Do you think most people can find true love on a dating app?
04. Have you (or someone you know) dated someone that you met on a dating app?
05. Why do a lot of people think using a dating app to find love is embarrassing?

Common Features

The Situation

Tinder has achieved international success in the dating market. It is used in more than 190 countries, and profiles on Tinder receive more than two billion views per day!

This is due in part to its straight-forward design, as well as its simple feature of swiping right if you like someone, and swiping left if you don't like someone.

With the success of Tinder, other companies decided to launch their own dating apps, with their own unique features.

Create a list of features you find in dating apps, as well as features you would like to find in dating apps.

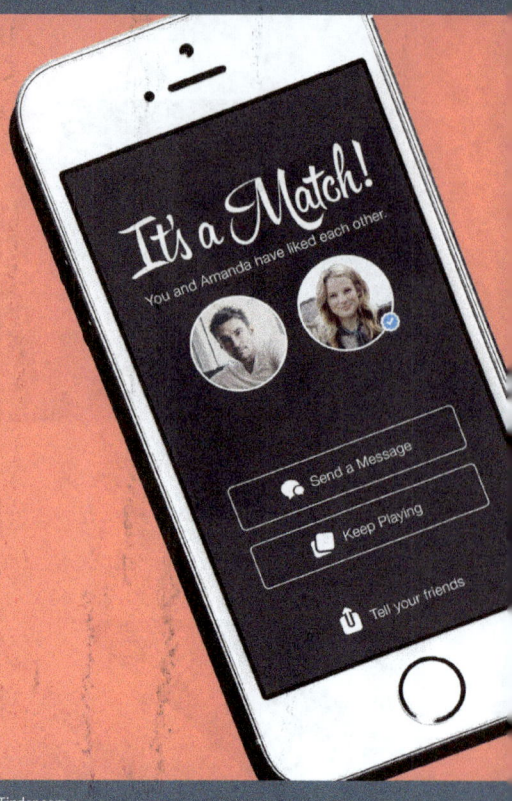

Images used with the permission of Tinder and Match.com. Information regarding Tinder from Tinder.com.

01. _____
02. _____
03. _____
04. _____
05. _____
06. _____
07. _____
08. _____
09. _____
10. _____

Pros and Cons

Making a Match

Discussion Activity

One feature that you can find in any dating app is the ability to apply filters. This means that you choose which type of people that you want to see, and which types of people you don't want to see.

What filters should be included in a dating app? What should the range or options be for each filter?

Example	
Age	18-24 / 25-30 / 31-35 / 36-40 / 41-50

01. _____   _____

02. _____   _____

03. _____   _____

04. _____   _____

05. _____   _____

06. _____   _____

07. _____   _____

08. _____   _____

09. _____   _____

10. _____   _____

Activity Discussion

Discuss the following questions with your group.

01. What would your choices be for each filter if you were using a dating app?
02. Which 3 filters are the most important to you?
03. Which 3 filters are the least important to you?

A New Dating App

Collaborative Activity

The dating app market is booming. Tinder and other dating apps have made billions of dollars, and you want a piece of that! You have decided to create your own dating app.

Answer the following questions.

01. Do users need to connect their profile to a social media site (Facebook, Google, etc.)?

02. What personal information are users required to give when they sign up?

03. What optional information can users provide about themselves?

04. What are the rules for pictures?

05. What free features will the app have?

06. What premium features can users purchase?

07. What type of subscription service will you offer?

08. How will users be matched?

09. What preferences can users filter and sort by?

Statistics and Discussion

The first Sunday of January is generally the busiest day for online dating. More people are motivated to find love due to New Year's resolutions (and the cold weather).[1]

One-in-five online daters have asked someone else to help them with their profile.[2]

One-third of people who have used online dating have never actually gone on a date with someone they met on these sites.[2]

Check "Statistics Sources" in the back of the workbook for additional information.

Statistics Discussion

Discuss the following questions with a partner.

01. Do people in your country feel pressured to be in a relationship during holidays?
02. Why do so many people end up not meeting anyone from a dating app?
03. Do you think it is helpful to ask someone to help you write a dating profile?

Agree or Disagree

Do you agree or disagree with the following statements?

01. Only desperate people use dating apps.
02. It's very unlikely for a relationship started on a dating app to be successful.
03. Dating apps are full of people trying to scam you.

Unit 25

Using Tablets Instead of Textbooks

What do you think are the pros and cons of using tablets instead of textbooks?

Vocabulary and Discussion

Crack

I accidentally dropped my phone and cracked the screen.

Resolution

My tablet's resolution is quite high. Pictures on it are clear and beautiful.

Overheat

Please take the dog inside. He's overheated from running in the sun.

Battery

Do you have a charger? My phone's battery drains too quickly.

Feature

One feature of the gaming system is wireless controllers.

Performance

My new hard drive's performance is much faster than my old one's.

Discussion Questions

Discuss the following questions with a partner. Be prepared to share your answers.

01. How do you think your school life would have been different if you had been able to use tablets in school?
02. If you were to study with a tablet, what features would you like?
03. What is your favorite app to use on your smartphone or tablet?
04. What apps do you think are useful for students?
05. What apps do you think are a distraction to students?

The Better Choice

Discussion Activity

What do you think is the best choice in each situation: a printed book or an e-book? Explain your reasons.

Reading with a child.

Reading in bed.

Sharing a book.

Reading while commuting.

Having a large selection.

Getting the book quickly.

Page 156 — Pros and Cons

A Tablet for Travel

Discussion Activity

You have a daily commute of one-hour to work, and you want to buy a tablet to make the commute more enjoyable. However, you also want to be able to use the tablet for work purposes, such as for conference calls and word processing. You are not rich, so it needs to be good value for the money. You are trying to decide between three budget tablets.

Which do you think is the best choice? Write your answer, and then compare it with a partner.

Choice A $125

12-hour battery life
4Mp back camera
1024x600 resolution
1.2GHz processor
128Gb storage capacity
Runs an older OS
May overheat

Choice B $230

8-hour battery life
8Mp back camera
1900x1200 resolution
2.4GHz processor
256Gb storage capacity
Runs a current OS
May have a battery problem

Choice C $199

10-hour battery life
4Mp front camera
1280x800 resolution
1.3GHz processor
256Gb storage capacity
Runs a current OS
Screen may easily crack

Using Tablets Instead of Textbooks

Designing a Tablet

Collaborative Activity

The Board of Education in your city has decided to provide every student in your school with a tablet to use during the school year. This tablet will be checked out from the school at the beginning of the year, and returned at the end of the year. It will be used for a minimum of three years. Since the school is testing the program, it doesn't want to spend a lot of money, so it needs to balance the cost of the table with features and performance. With this in mind, the Board of Education has given you a budget of **$200 per tablet**.

Work with a partner or group to design a suitable tablet from the options below. Circle each option.

	Budget Options $10 each	Mid-range Options $25 each	Premium Options $35 each
01. Screen Size	8.4 inches	10 inches	12.4 inches
02. Resolution	1920x1200	2560x1600	3000x2000
03. Weight	0.7kg	0.5kg	0.4kg
04. Processor Speed	1.6GHz	2.0GHz	2.4GHz
05. Storage Capacity	128Gb	256Gb	512Gb
06. RAM	4Gb	8Gb	16Gb
07. Back Camera	6Mp	8Mp	16Mp
08. Front Camera	4Mp	5Mp	8Mp
09. Battery Life	8 hours	11 hours	14 hours
10. Android OS	Previous version		Current version
11. Word Processor	Previous version		Current version

Total Cost: _____

Pros and Cons

Statistics and Discussion

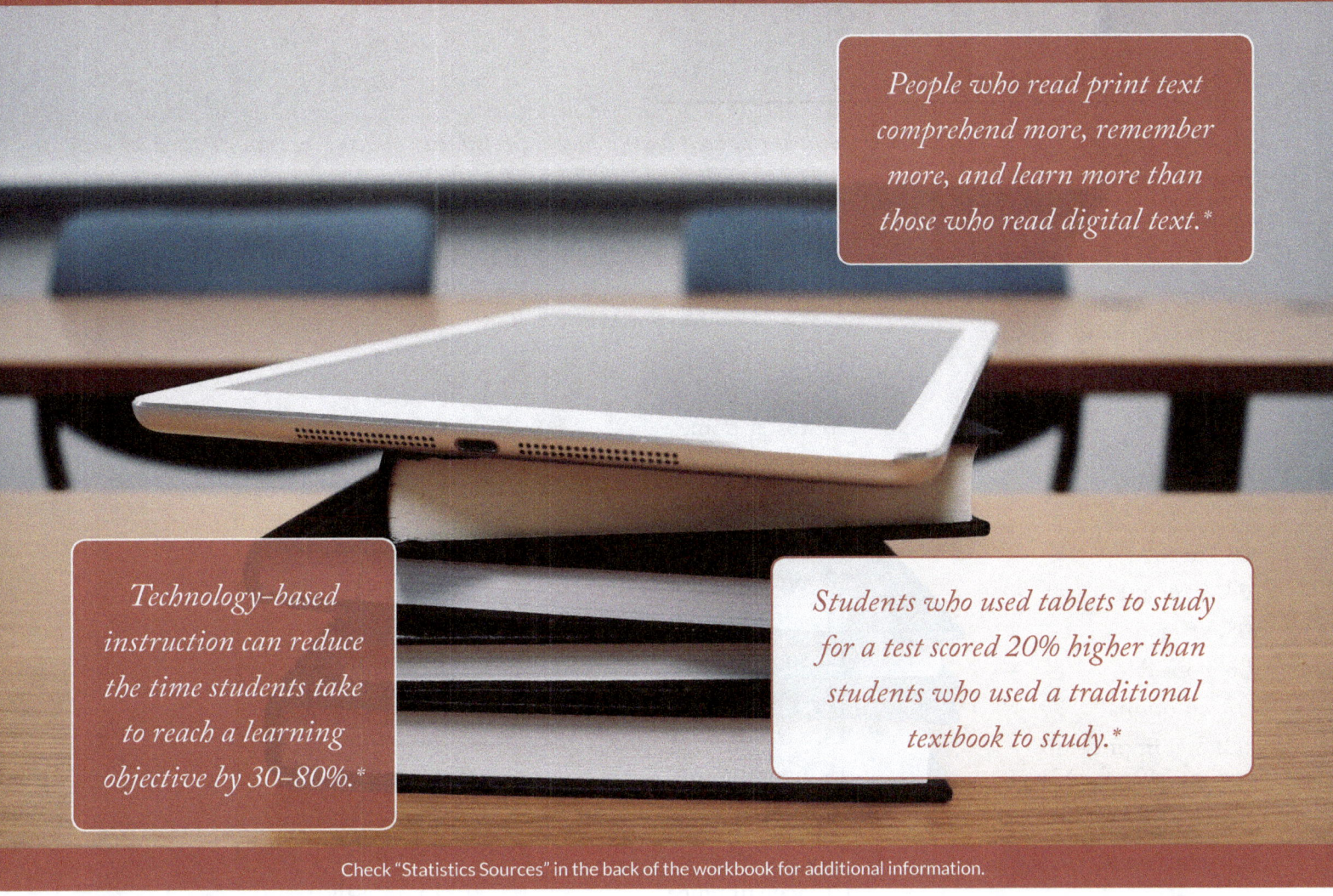

*People who read print text comprehend more, remember more, and learn more than those who read digital text.**

*Technology-based instruction can reduce the time students take to reach a learning objective by 30-80%.**

*Students who used tablets to study for a test scored 20% higher than students who used a traditional textbook to study.**

Check "Statistics Sources" in the back of the workbook for additional information.

Statistics Discussion

Discuss the following questions with a partner.

01. Why do you think students may learn faster when using tablets?
02. If people who read print text learn and comprehend more, why do students who use tablets score higher on tests?
03. Do these statistics influence how you think schools should use technology in classrooms?

Extended Discussion

Discuss the following questions with a partner.

01. Should parents or the schools be required to provide tablets for students?
02. Are you concerned about any health risks for children from using tablets more?
03. Which subjects are poorly suited for tablets, and which are ideally suited for them?

Vocabulary Bank

A Note on the Vocabulary

At the beginning of each unit, the six words introduced have a higher probability of being new to students, or may be used more frequently within that unit. However, there may be other words within the unit that are new, or have multiple meanings that may lead to some confusion for students. The six words from the beginning of each unit, as well as any potentially tricky words, will be listed here, so that students may preview them before class, or so that the teacher can preteach them at the beginning of the class. Some words are listed twice, as some teachers may choose to teach the units out of order.

Unit 01

01. abusive
02. acceptable
03. arrange
04. arrogant
05. attraction
06. consider
07. emotional
08. first impression
09. legal
10. mental
11. motivate
12. passion
13. personality
14. physical
15. potential
16. stable
17. stranger
18. threaten
19. zodiac sign

Unit 02

01. abduct
02. beggar
03. citizen
04. extended family
05. foreclose
06. foster home
07. homeless shelter
08. low-income
09. paycheck-to-paycheck
10. poverty
11. situation
12. soup kitchen
13. spouse
14. survive
15. unemployed

Unit 03

01. acquaintance
02. betray
03. concept
04. dating profile
05. exaggerate
06. fib
07. hang out
08. pull over
09. resumé
10. social media
11. tactful

Unit 04

01. ally
02. capable
03. casualty
04. counterattack
05. declare
06. embargo
07. enemy
08. evidence
09. individual
10. knock out
11. launch an attack
12. might
13. military
14. punish
15. rapidly
16. sanction
17. serve a country
18. unrest
19. violate

Unit 05

01. abandon
02. accident
03. adjust
04. beat
05. disabled
06. enroll
07. genes
08. injure

09. orphan
10. orphanage
11. rebuild
12. recover
13. resistant
14. scar
15. timid

Unit 06

01. agriculture
02. asteroid
03. astronaut
04. biodome
05. botanist
06. cargo
07. civilization
08. colony
09. dinosaur
10. engineer
11. laborer
12. landscape
13. microscopic
14. organism
15. permanent
16. rover
17. self-sustaining
18. space shuttle
19. venue

Unit 07

01. aging population
02. arrest
03. birthrate
04. boost
05. come up with
06. condition
07. council
08. courtship
09. dwindle
10. face a problem
11. fertility
12. gender
13. imbalance
14. imbalance
15. impact
16. notable
17. overpopulation
18. policy
19. resources
20. revenue
21. sneak
22. spoiled
23. violate
24. win someone's heart

Unit 08

01. build a family
02. chores
03. cohabitation
04. compatibility
05. exception
06. income
07. interracial
08. interreligious
09. minimum wage
10. permit
11. socialize
12. society
13. take turns

Unit 09

01. ban
02. break up
03. colleague
04. commission
05. company policy
06. deal with someone
07. decent
08. employee evaluation
09. gossip
10. let someone go
11. promotion
12. similar
13. supervisor

Unit 10

01. adjust
02. care package
03. developed
04. emigrate
05. flavor
06. ideal
07. immigrate
08. migrate
09. permanent
10. potential
11. public welfare
12. quality
13. risk
14. senior citizen
15. stick out
16. welfare

Unit 11

01. adventurous
02. calculate
03. charity
04. childfree

Vocabulary Bank

05. daycare
06. get around
07. inherit
08. inheritance
09. retire
10. retirement community
11. retirement plan
12. romantic partner
13. rv
14. social activities
15. suitable
16. will

Unit 12

01. attempt
02. clone
03. consume
04. deceased
05. dinosaur
06. endangered
07. extinct
08. furious
09. gene
10. laboratory
11. organ
12. separate
13. species
14. spouse
15. transplant

Unit 13

01. consequence
02. course content
03. discourage
04. fault
05. focus

06. freshman
07. high school sweetheart
08. junior
09. principal
10. secret crush
11. semester
12. senior
13. sophomore
14. syllabus
15. transfer

Unit 14

01. allowance
02. bed linens
03. calculate
04. chores
05. earn
06. generation
07. groceries
08. high marks
09. invest
10. percentage
11. purchase
12. rule of thumb
13. semester
14. teenager

Unit 15

01. accomplish
02. addiction
03. campaign
04. deal with
05. drop out of
06. fit in
07. give up something
08. launch

09. media
10. nicotine gum
11. nicotine patch
12. on the wrong track
13. peer pressure
14. promote
15. public area
16. rebellious
17. related
18. skip school
19. stop cold turkey
20. stroke
21. typical

Unit 16

01. approximately
02. be wiped out
03. cycle
04. drought
05. emissions
06. functional
07. gas
08. impact
09. infrastructure
10. leisure activities
11. malaria
12. open-air market
13. petrol
14. populace
15. relocate
16. unbreathable

Unit 17

01. arsenal
02. bury
03. cannon

04. coal
05. disarm
06. evacuate
07. facility
08. generate
09. launch
10. meltdown
11. poison
12. power plant
13. retaliate

Unit 18

01. asylum
02. diverse
03. emigrate
04. fade away
05. foundation
06. immigrate
07. integrate
08. populate
09. pure
10. recipient
11. unique

Unit 19

01. adjust
02. bride
03. compromise
04. contradict
05. critical
06. currently
07. groom
08. interracial
09. merge
10. native
11. negative

12. positive
13. push someone
14. raise a child
15. spouse
16. wed

Unit 20

01. arson
02. assault
03. blackmail
04. DUI
05. endanger
06. fine
07. first degree murder
08. guilty
09. gun-control
10. harsh
11. hit and run
12. homicide
13. incarceration
14. innocent
15. investigate
16. kidnapping
17. legal system
18. litter
19. major crime
20. manslaughter
21. minor crime
22. monitor
23. on the rise
24. qualified
25. rape
26. rehabilitate
27. severe
28. shoplifting
29. speeding

Unit 21

01. attracted to
02. build a future
03. consequence
04. fee
05. graduate
06. interaction
07. long-term
08. passion
09. penalty
10. policy
11. semester
12. short-term
13. threaten
14. training school

Unit 22

01. aspect
02. doomed
03. entrepreneur
04. expand
05. founder
06. march
07. parade
08. sacrifice
09. savings
10. scale a business
11. significantly
12. start-up
13. to have what it takes

Unit 23

01. abuse
02. counseling
03. course
04. decline

Vocabulary Bank

05. equality
06. impact
07. infidelity
08. intimacy
09. negative
10. positive
11. property
12. separate
13. upwards trend
14. victim

Unit 24

01. booming
02. chemistry
03. desperate
04. feature
05. filter
06. match
07. premium
08. profile
09. profile views
10. range
11. resolution
12. scam
13. social media
14. sort
15. straight-forward
16. subscription
17. swipe
18. tap

Unit 25

01. balance
02. battery life
03. charger
04. check out

05. commute
06. comprehend
07. conference call
08. crack
09. digital
10. distraction
11. drain
12. feature
13. operating system
14. overheat
15. performance
16. processor
17. RAM
18. screen resolution
19. selection
20. storage capacity
21. tablet
22. value for the money
23. wireless
24. word processing

Statistics Sources

A Tip on the Statistics

I like statistics, and I often say that statistics don't lie. Sure, they can be manipulated, misinterpreted, misrepresented, cherry-picked, etc., but those tend to be issues of human-error and prejudice rather than a problem with the statistics themselves. Admittedly, some of these sources may be from people with their own biases and agendas, but the point of the statistics is to get the students discussing different viewpoints, and looking at things from a different angle. So, take them with a grain of salt.

With that said, some of these topics in this book are a bit serious, and sometimes students become a bit passionate in their opinions, so I always preface class by telling students to put feelings aside, because we feel based on how we've been taught to feel, and sometimes our preconceptions may be incorrect. Look at the statistics without emotion, and interpret them without prejudice. Think critically, and challenge your perception of the world. With this framework in mind, students tend to perform better in class, and get more from it, because they are primed to receive new ideas.

Set the framework before class, and your students will reap the benefits.

Statistic Sources

Unit 01	www.statisticbrain.com/arranged-marriage-statistics
Unit 02	1. www.bbc.com/news/av/uk-33729544/only-one-in-five-beggars-homeless-in-england-and-wales 2. blogs.wsj.com/indiarealtime/2012/10/16/indias-missing-children-by-the-numbers 3. 2001-2009.state.gov/g/tip/rls/tiprpt/2008/105379.htm
Unit 03	www.brandongaille.com/24-nose-growing-statistics-on-lying
Unit 04	en.wikipedia.org/wiki/war
Unit 05	www.thelaboroflove.com/articles/child-adoption-statistics-around-the-world
Unit 06	en.wikipedia.org/wiki/Colonization_of_Mars
Unit 07	en.wikipedia.org/wiki/One-child_policy
Unit 08	1. https://www.thespruce.com/cohabitation-facts-and-statistics-2302236 2. www.theatlantic.com/health/archive/2014/03/the-science-of-cohabitation-a-step-toward-marriage-not-a-rebellion/284512/
Unit 09	Horan, S. M., & Chory, R. M. (2011) Understanding work-life blending: Credibility implications for those who date at work.
Unit 10	www.oecd.org
Unit 11	Ellen Walker, Ph.D. Complete Without Kids: An Insider's Guide to Childfree Living By Choice Or By Chance.
Unit 12	www.someinterestingfacts.net/facts-about-cloning

Unit 13	1. www.rebelcircus.com/blog/surprising-statistics-high-school-sweethearts 2. www.childtrends.org/indicators/dating
Unit 14	1. www.kidsmoney.org/allstats.htm 2. www.moneycrashers.com/allowance-kids-chores
Unit 15	1. http://english.jschina.com.cn/20322/201611/t3110842.shtml 2. https://www.verywellmind.com/global-smoking-statistics-for-2002-2824393 3. http://www.who.int/news-room/fact-sheets/detail/tobacco
Unit 16	1. www.statista.com/topics/1148/global-climate-change 2. www.who.int/news-room/fact-sheets/detail/climate-change-and-health
Unit 17	www.newint.org/features/2008/06/01/nuclear-weapons-facts
Unit 18	gmdac.iom.int/global-migration-trends-factsheet
Unit 19	en.wikipedia.org/wiki/Interracial_marriage
Unit 20	1. en.wikipedia.org/wiki/List_of_countries_by_intentional_homicide_rate 2. en.wikipedia.org/wiki/List_of_countries_by_incarceration_rate
Unit 21	en.wikipedia.org/wiki/sexual_harassment_in_education_in_the_united_states
Unit 22	www.inc.com/thomas-koulopoulos/5-of-the-most-surprising-statistics-about-start-ups.html
Unit 23	1. www.divorcestatistics.org 2. en.wikipedia.org/wiki/Divorce#Statistics
Unit 24	1. www.datingsitesreviews.com/staticpages/index.php?page=Online-Dating-Industry-Facts-Statistics 2. http://www.pewresearch.org/fact-tank/2016/02/29/5-facts-about-online-dating/
Unit 25	www.tablets-textbooks.procon.org